# Las Maquiladoras:
# Assembly and Manufacturing Plants
# on the United States-Mexico Border

## An International Guide

# Las Maquiladoras: Assembly and Manufacturing Plants on the United States-Mexico Border

## An International Guide

Martin H. Sable

The Haworth Press
New York • London

*Las Maquiladoras: Assembly and Manufacturing Plants on the United States-Mexico Border: An International Guide*, has also been published as *Behavioral & Social Sciences Librarian*, Volume 7, Numbers 3/4 1989.

The Haworth Press, Inc., 10 Alice Street, Binghamton, NY 13904-1580
EUROSPAN/Haworth, 3 Henrietta Street, London WC2E 8LU England

**Library of Congress Cataloging-in-Publication Data**

Sable, Martin Howard.
    Las Maquiladoras : assembly and manufacturing plants on the United States-Mexico border : an international guide / Martin H. Sable.
        p.   cm.
    Most of the items were published in English and Spanish: also contains works published in French, German, Italian, and Portuguese.
    "Has also been published as Behavioral & social sciences librarian, volume 7, numbers 3/4 1989" — T.p. verso.
    Includes indexes.
    ISBN 0-86656-904-9
    1. Offshore assembly industry — Mexican-American Border Region — Bibliography. 2. Offshore assembly industry — Mexican-American Border Region — Directories. I. Title.
Z7914.M3S23        1989
[HD9734.M43M49]
338.4'767'09721 — dc20
                                                                                                    89-32394
                                                                                                    CIP

THIS BOOK IS DEDICATED TO
MY PARENTS-IN-LAW

REBECCA GIBBS  SAMUEL GIBBS
(1893-1963)   (1883-1953)

OF WEST ROXBURY, MASSACHUSETTS

# Las Maquiladoras: Assembly and Manufacturing Plants on the United States-Mexico Border

## An International Guide

## CONTENTS

## DISCLAIMER STATEMENT

All information in this book is furnished as a matter of service only. While efforts have been made to include correct, current information, no guarantee is given nor should any be inferred with regard to accuracy and/or timeliness of any and all data contained herein.

The publishers and the officers, agents and employees thereof, as well as the compiler of the material, make no warranties, express or implied, representations or promises whatsoever concerning the individuals, firms, institutions, labor organizations, professional associations, information centers, research centers, agents and departments of any government at any and all levels, chambers of commerce, and business associations, and any and all entities referred to, listed or named, or for the services rendered thereby. The publisher and the officers, agents and employees thereof, as well as the compiler, shall not be liable for any damages whatsoever arising from any errors or omissions made in the compiling or printing of this book.

# ABOUT THE AUTHOR

**Martin H. Sable,** Professor, School of Library and Information Science, University of Wisconsin-Milwaukee, is an expert on Latin American Studies. He has published 55 journal articles and 25 book-length reference works, the latter mainly in Latin American Studies, including *Mexican and Mexican-American Agricultural Labor in the United States: An International Bibliography* (The Haworth Press, 1987). Some of his Latin American Studies titles are standards in the field and used by academicians, government and business experts, and researchers worldwide.

Dr. Sable is a founding member of the Latin American Studies Association and a member of the Conference on Latin American History and of many library organizations. He serves on the board of the Midwest Association for Latin American Studies and has been Advisory Editor on *Latin America for The Encyclopedia Americana* since 1967. Dr. Sable founded the newsletter of the Pacific Coast Council on Latin American Studies.

He holds a B.A. degree in Romance Languages, M.A. and M.S. degrees respectively in Latin American Studies and Library Science, and a doctorate degree in Spanish.

# I. The Maquiladora:
# Its Origins, Qualities and Implications

When they were first introduced along the U.S.-Mexican border in the 1960s, *maquiladoras* were assembly plants, where American components were assembled by Mexican minimum-wage unskilled workers, typically young women, into products then reshipped into the American market. The Mexican and United States governments agreed on reduced tariffs for entry of components into Mexico, and of finished products into the United States, for their mutual benefit: jobs, however low-paying, for Mexicans, and a source of low-cost labor for American firms, beset by competition from foreign products offered at extremely competitive prices in the United States. And while many American manufacturers have set up assembly and manufacturing plants in other low-wage offshore regions of the world, notably the Far East and South Pacific (Philippines), none of these regions has the built-in "next door neighbor" advantage, resulting in minimal transportation charges that location on the Mexican border permits. And whereas the present bibliography focuses upon the region of Mexico inside the border with the United States, it should be noted that the Caribbean in general has, since the 1960s, engaged in manufacturing activities for United States firms. In some instances, such as the highly publicized "Operation Bootstrap" in Puerto Rico (begun optimistically but subsequently experiencing doubtful results), tax incentives motivated plant installation, while in others such as subcontract clothing production in Colombian factories, the stimulus provided was the traditional cheap labor. That additional Caribbean nations increasingly come under serious study, with respect to the present topic, is indicated by D. Kelly's article, "St. Lucia's Female Electronics Factory Workers: Key Components in an Export-Oriented Industrialization Strategy" (*World Development*, volume 14, number 7, July 1986, pages 823-838).

Despite the entry of United States manufacturers into the various geographic regions cited above, the U.S.-Mexico Border remains the favorite area. Proximity, low labor and trans-shipment costs, long experience in Mexico (for many firms), and two cooperative governments fostering border industrialization (the United States Government offers tax incentives), represent factors that taken together render the border region *the* prime manufacturing location choice.

In discussing border labor conditions, it is appropriate to check the *1988-1989 Texas Almanac and State Industrial Guide* (Dallas: *Morning News*; Austin: distributed by Texas Monthly Press, 1987). On pages 411-412 we learn that despite the drop in retail sales of American products to Mexicans who regularly cross the border to shop, the border's overall economic strength is growing, and jobs along the border have been increasing, by comparison with former periods. For example, rates of increase in McAllen, El Paso, and Laredo as of 1987 were 4%, 3%, and 2%, respectively. Despite these statistics, however, border cities on the Texas side suffer the highest rate of unemployment in that state. McAllen, Texas, for example, had a 20% unemployment average during 1986.

What of the need for *maquiladora* workers? The *Guide* states that during 1984-1985, there was a surge in the number of such employees working in "twin-plants" on the Mexican side, and despite the falling value of the Mexican peso, these workers continued to cross the border for shopping in Texas border cities.

The Spanish word *maquiladora* comes from the verb *maquilar*, which one might translate as the miller's receiving corn (grain) as payment for grinding corn for others. The American firms bring in the "grain" in the form of the components (and the payment of Mexican wages), Mexican labor does the "grinding" and the finished product ("the ground corn") returns to the U.S. market. What types of products are these? Automobiles and parts, electrical appliances, electronics, computers, clothing, cosmetics, pharmaceuticals, and a host of others, produced by some of the largest, medium-sized and small U.S. industrial firms.

And while the cry has arisen, especially from labor unions, that "runaway" plants have stripped American workers of hundreds of thousands of jobs, the fact remains that on the whole American manufacturers have, as a result of setting up *maquiladoras*, been able to withstand intense foreign competition in their own market while simultaneously aiding the Mexican economy (on which the U.S. depends as a source for nearby petroleum).

Sociological studies have also been done on the *maquiladoras'* impact on Mexican female labor; some female workers charge underpayment. One might logically counter this charge with the question: had the *maquiladoras* never existed, what might have been the wages paid to this young, inexperienced, unskilled female labor by potential (typically non-existent) Mexican industry in the hitherto less industrialized Mexican border areas? Negating this argument are studies (cited herein) of female labor exploitation, with resulting strikes against some *maquiladoras*.

Additional advantages of the *maquiladora* accrue because of its unique "city-twinning" nature: while the assembly plant is located just across the U.S.-Mexican border in Mexico, its administrative headquarters are situated on the U.S. side, where administrative and logistical staff oversee all non-manufacturing aspects of the "foreign operation" a few miles distant. The result: the two cities are bound together, rather than being isolated, and a "fraternal spirit" is initiated, whereby differences of whatever type tend to subside in favor of an emphasis on common traits and similarities. As long ago as the year 1965, the Mexican Government inaugurated a Border Industrialization Program for the city of Tijuana, Mexico, just across the border from San Diego. This "twinning" of cities, as a result of the *maquiladoras* established in Tijuana (with their corresponding headquarters in San Diego), stimulated economic activities of a wide variety in both cities. They also had a positive impact on the health, welfare and educational facilities in northern Baja California as a result of the increased concern produced within the hundreds of American firms that have, since 1965, established *maquiladoras* in Tijuana and Mexicali (whose American "twin" is Calexico, California). Similar situations obtain all along the U.S.-Mexican border: Nogales, Arizona, and Nogales, Mexico; and the Texas cities of Brownsville with Matamoros, Mexico; Del Rio with Ciudad Acuña; El Paso with Ciudad Juarez; Laredo with Nuevo Laredo; McAllen with Reynosa; and Eagle Pass with Piedras Negras.

Volume 2 of the third edition of *Cities of the World* (Detroit: Gale Research Company, 1987) presents two examples of such "twin" cities. On page 545 in treating El Paso, Texas and Ciudad Juarez, Mexico, it states:

> Under Mexico's border industrialization program, designed to raise the standard of living along the entire border, a large number of industrial plants, many of them wholly owned subsidiaries of American firms, have been established to take advantage of low labor costs. The 'twin-plant' concept, with factories in Ciudad Juarez performing labor-intensive work in cooperation with mechanized operations in their counterpart plants in the United States, and has developed industrial links between this city and El Paso, Texas, just across the border.

On pages 549-550 of the same volume, we learn of some of the products manufactured in the *maquiladoras* located in Matamoros, Mexico, on the opposite side of the border from Brownsville, Texas:

> Matamoros developed principally as an agricultural processing center, and agribusiness is still the area's largest employer and income-earner. In recent years, some 50 border industries have been established here, ranging from electronics, chemicals, and plastics industries to textile and garment plants. Large-scale heavy industry is still lacking, but further development of the city's potential as a processor, entrepôt, and communications hub is expected.

*Maquiladoras* and their phenomenal growth comprised one segment of the "McNeil-Lehrer News Hour," televised from 6 to 7 p.m., Central Standard Time, over Channel 11 (Chicago), of the Public Broadcasting System, on August 8, 1986. Among the facts provided: Japanese and other foreign firms are now locating their plants on the Mexican side of the border because labor costs there are among the lowest in the world; unskilled females comprise the workers; and the juxtaposition of low-cost labor adjacent to the world's largest market, the United States, is attractive. As of 1985, about 700 *maquiladoras* provided employment for some 250,000

Mexican workers. Interviewed on the program was Howard Boysen, of the IMEC Corporation, San Diego, California, a firm that sets up *maquiladoras* for manufacturers. Boysen claims that based upon economic factors involved, the future growth of *maquiladoras* is so rapid as to be incalculable.

Public Broadcasting Service television Channel 11 (Chicago), as recently as on June 8, 1988, from 10:00-11:00 p.m. telecast a program entitled "Mexamerica," one segment in a series entitled "The Nine Nations of North America," based upon Joel Garreau's 1981 book of the same title. Much of this program was devoted to the topic of border studies in general. It was pointed out that *maquiladoras* have, during the 1980s, penetrated several hundred miles south of the border into northern Mexico. Viewers witnessed dozens of young Mexican women engaged in the production of electronic parts at the Chihuahua (city) plant of Honeywell, some 400 miles from the border. Joel Garreau, the author who also acted as TV host, stated that whereas an average unemployment rate of 40% exists in other Mexican regions, Chihuahua (city) has only a 4% rate. And while U.S. industry does penetrate southward from the border, the existence of a blending of Mexican and U.S. cultures on the border is not only apparent to the inhabitants, but additionally it attracts the attention of experts in a myriad of disciplines.

A subsequent television program dealing in part with *maquiladoras* was entitled "Mexico's Crisis: A Special Report," one in the weekly series, "Adam Smith's Money World," telecast over the Public Broadcasting Service's affiliated station in Milwaukee, Wisconsin, Channel 10, on July 3, 1988, from 4:30-5:00 p.m. Echoing the notion of the penetration of the *maquiladora* far south of the border, and citing Monterrey, Mexico, as an example, Larry Keith, the program's narrator, stated that according to latest figures there were (as of 1988) 1,400 *maquiladoras* employing approximately 360,000 workers. These figures obviously confirm the December 12, 1987, *Los Angeles Times* report according to which U.S. and Mexican border state governors agreed on industrialization and economic development of the border region as their top priority over drug enforcement. These 1988 statistics also indicate a 100% increase in the number of *maquiladoras* in existence, and a 30%-plus rise in the number of persons employed by them, by comparison with the 1986 figures for *maquiladoras* and their workers, cited in the McNeil-Lehrer telecast of August 8, 1986.

Anthropologists, business and economics experts, geographers, historians, political scientists, language specialists, sociologists, folklorists, agronomists and Mexicanists, have developed an interdisciplinary field of border studies, and have established the Association of Borderlands Scholars. The Association cooperated in organizing the 34th annual meeting of the Pacific Coast Council on Latin American Studies, held at the Universidad Autónoma de Baja California, in Mexicali, Mexico from October 20-23, 1988. The majority of the panels and sessions dealt with the culture, geography, history, literature and politics of the Mexican borderlands; one session was entitled "Microeconomics of Máquila Operations," while the panel on "Mexico: Economics and Foreign Trade" included a paper entitled "The Economic Impact of the Maquiladora Industry: The Texas Experience."

As a result of scholarly interest in Border Studies and Mexico in general, all campuses of the University of California are cooperating with Mexican educational institutions, in a variety of disciplines, within the University of California Consortium on Mexico and the United States. The Consortium's headquarters are located at the University of California, Riverside, and its first Director, Dr. Arturo Gomez-Pompa, Director of the Flora of Mexico Program at the National Research Institute of Biotic Resources at Jalapa, Veracruz, on January 15, 1986, joined the faculty of Botany and Plant Sciences at Riverside. The University of Texas at Austin also supports a Mexico-United States Border Studies Program. The University of Texas at El Paso promotes teaching and research regarding the U.S.-Mexican border through its Center for Inter-American and Border Studies.

In its issue of January 19, 1986 (section III, page 4, column 3), the *New York Times* reported that the Mexican Government, after some 20 years' experience with *maquiladoras*, considers them to be a significant element in its economic rehabilitation program, and aims to attract more American firms into establishing them. Especially since 1980, the term *maquiladora* also encompasses the complete production process, as opposed to mere assembly of components. In order to encourage the entry of American firms, the *New*

*York Times* stated that Mexico was providing American firms access to Mexican consumers as well as labor, in contrast to the original provisos that permitted only duty-free entry of materials, and required the export of all finished products from Mexico.

Competition from many foreign nations, including France, Japan and The Netherlands, exists in the establishment of *maquiladoras*, according to Melita Garza's article titled "Wisconsin Firms Head South, But Their Mexican Plants Cause Controversy" (*Milwaukee Journal*, "Business," Section D., December 14, 1986, pp. 1D, 4D). An article printed in early 1988 added Canada to the group, and the end is not in sight. Besides citing a three-day conference held in Acapulco in early December of 1986, attended by over 350 U.S. businessmen on the topic of *maquiladoras*, the article also pointed out that 70% of materials used in *maquiladora* production is of U.S. origin, whereas the U.S. content is far less for products manufactured in similar plant facilities in the Far East. In her concluding section, Garza reported that *maquiladoras* have replaced the tourist industry as Mexico's second most important source of foreign exchange. Perhaps the *maquiladora* concept, sufficiently expanded, will over a period of years help to solve Mexico's economic problems while simultaneously allowing American firms to meet foreign competition. (Opposing this attitude are experts who claim that hand-to-mouth wages paid to *maquiladora* employees ultimately are worthless in helping to reduce the overall negative condition of Mexico's economy.)

In a second article on the same page, entitled "Former Governor Urges State Firms to Mexico," the same author stated that former Wisconsin Governor and former U.S. Ambassador to Mexico, Patrick Lucey, had assisted some U.S. firms in establishing *maquiladoras*. In the interview Governor Lucey bemoaned the annual downward trend in real income for most Mexicans, and the consequent reduction of some Mexican political and economic stability. While favoring the establishment of a U.S.-Canadian-Mexican common market, Lucey believes that in order to avert a Mexican crisis, a plan suggested by Felix G. Rohatyn and Roger C. Altman, (respectively a general partner in the investment firm of Lazard Frères & Company of New York and ex-Assistant Secretary of the Treasury), and involving the U.S. Government, the World Bank, the Japanese Government, and private U.S. and Mexican citizens, be implemented. Basically, their plan calls for a temporary U.S.-Mexican development finance program. In Lucey's words: "Ultimately, only that kind of program, triggering $20 billion to $30 billion of direct investment for Mexico and several million new jobs, will stunt a political and economic disaster."

Marshall McLuhan's global village has become a cliché, overly repeated perhaps because its truth is reconfirmed daily. It is stated that division of labor has already become internationalized; and while multinational corporations, located on all continents, have been recognized for decades as rivalling smaller nations in economic strength, only in the mid-1980s has attention been directed to the strength of corporate and individual wealth, also operating internationally. And in consideration of the continuing and massive entry into the United States of Mexicans and Central Americans, of the existence of *maquiladoras* and of the commonality of the "border culture," there are suggestions of a Mexican-United States-Canadian common market. Dare we supposed what the 21st century may hold?

To experts in the field of Future Studies, to Mexicanists, to my fellow Latinamericanists, and to all others concerned directly or indirectly with any aspect of the *maquiladora*, I offer the hope that the present source might be of assistance.

*Martin H. Sable*

## ABBREVIATIONS UTILIZED IN THE BIBLIOGRAPHY

a. — annual
comp. — compiler
D.F. — Federal District, Mexico City
ed. — editor, edition
Ed. — Editorial (publishing house)
GPO — U.S. Government Printing Office
Impr. — Imprenta (printing shop)
m. — monthly
n.d. — no date given
n.p. — no place given

p., pp. — pages
q. — quarterly
rev. — revised
s.a. — semi-annual
v. — volume(s)
v.p. — variously paged
·w. — weekly

# II. Use of the Guide

## DEFINITION, PURPOSE, ARRANGEMENT, CONTENT, TOPICS COVERED, AND USERS

*Las Maquiladoras* . . . is a combination bibliography and directory focusing upon a binational, shared production activity uniquely developed during the latter third of the 20th century. The bibliography is comprised of books and chapters of books, pamphlets, conference papers and proceedings, master's theses and doctoral dissertations, government publications, articles from scholarly journals, newspapers and popular-interest magazines, and videotapes of television programs. The earliest publications bear a 1960 issue date, while the most recent is a summer 1988 videotape. While most of the items were published in English and Spanish, the bibliography also contains works published in French, German, Italian and Portuguese. For each entry, full bibliographic data are presented, except for major journal titles issued in the United States; for these, place of publication is not given. However, for little-known journals and newspapers (and especially for alternative-press titles), U.S. cities are presented for purposes of identification and acquisition. All publications of any type published outside of the United States have their full bibliographic information presented, as do non-periodical (book-type) items issued in the United States. *Las Maquiladoras* . . . aims to provide students, researchers, librarians, international trade specialists and banks and government agencies basic research sources (and by means of its directories, alternative approaches to information) concerning *maquiladoras* and applied topics. The work is arranged chronologically by year, and within each year by month and date. As a result, users may trace events as they have occurred with the passage of time and study developments in a logical sequence.

The major sections of the work are arranged in the following sequence: I. The Maquiladoras: Its Origins, Qualities and Implications; II., Use of the Guide; III., the Bibliography; IV., Author Index; V., Subject Index; VI., Directories Section; VII., Index to Directories section. In the Bibliography as well as in the Author Index, when no author's name is given, the title of the work appears in its place; in addition, the names of business firms, government agencies, social service organizations and trade unions appear as corporate authors, together with names of persons as authors. Within the Index to Directories Section, the name of the specific entity/individual appears first, followed by U.S. state or foreign country of location. In this Index, all Spanish-language entities are located in Mexico. All numbers in all Indexes refer to entry numbers in the body of the work, and not to page numbers.

The *maquiladora*'s unique makeup renders it an attractive research topic. As an industrial entity it has existed since the mid-1960s. The topic, then, is a comparatively recent one, in terms of writings, and a goodly number of the listed items are from business and general-interest journal and magazine articles, as opposed to full-length books. While the thrust of the items included in the select bibliography has been upon the industrial, commercial and financial aspects of the phenomenon, including the actions of multinational corporations and their investments, there are also entries dealing with the matter of labor, United States and Mexican governmental undertakings, legal and urban problems, regional development and planning, population, technology transfer, socio-cultural considerations, and the interdisciplinary field known as Border Studies, which is concerned with a host of topics ranging from health and education, to urban geography, economic matters and the cultural impact on border residents (on both sides), of the establishment of *maquiladoras*. The impact on border culture, of economic development, industrialization and urbanization is also reflected.

In addition to users mentioned previously, this sourcebook should be of assistance to executives of business firms planning to establish *maquiladoras*, to professors of international trade, to economists and bankers concerned with Mexican industry, to those studying technology transfer as well as Mexican regional development and planning, and experts in most aspects of the interdisciplinary field of U.S.-Mexico Border Studies. The work is up to date as of spring, 1988. Finally, the business organizations, government agencies at various levels, information centers, labor unions, professional associations, research centers, and the roster of experts following the Subject Index represent, *in toto*, a directory that should provide much supplementary material to what appears in the bibliography.

# III. Bibliography

## 1960

**1**
"Big Companies Think Small When Moving into Mexico." *Business Week*, December 24, 1960, pp. 56-58.

## 1962

**2**
Beteta, M. R.
"Foreign Investments Wanted." *International Commerce* 68, September 3, 1962, pp. 19-20.

## 1964

**3**
México. Secretaría de Hacienda y Crédito Público
*Los Estímulos Fiscales y las Ayudas Financieras para la Exportación de Productos Manufacturados*. México, Dirección General de Estudios Hacendados, 1964.

## 1965

**4**
D'Antonio, William V., & Form, William H.
*Influentials in Two Border Cities: A Study in Community Decision-Making*. Notre Dame, IN, University of Notre Dame Press, 1965, 273p.

**5**
Titchener, W.
"Borderline Advantage: Tax Exemptions are Helping to Lure U.S. Firms to Mexico." *Barron's* 45, January 18, 1965, p. 9.

**6**

Tomlinson, E.
"Boomland South of the Border." *Reader's Digest* 86, March 1965, pp. 201-202.


**7**

Ceceña, J. L.
"Las Inversiones Extranjeras Directas en México." México, *Investigaciones Económicas* (98: 1), April-June 1965, pp. 271-299.


**8**

McCleneghan, T. J., & Gildersleeve, C. R.
"Paired Cities on the Arizona-Sonora Border." *Arizona Review* 14, June 1965, pp. 9-13.


**9**

Valle, C. della
"Il Recente Sviluppo Economica e Demografico del Messico." Rome, *Bolletino della Societá Geografica Italiana* (6: 11-12), November-December 1965, pp. 587-611.


*1966*

**10**

Ortega Mata, R.
"Una Metodología para la Planificación del Desarrollo Económico y Social Regional de México." México, *Revista Mexicana de Sociología* (28: 3), July-September 1966, pp. 551-569.


*1967*

**11**

Palacios, Fausto E., & Montiel, Guillermo
*Industrialización del Estado de Baja California*. México, Banco de Comercio, 1967.

**12**
Perez Lopez, E. et al.
*Mexico's Recent Economic Growth; the Mexican View*. Austin, TX, University of Texas Press, 1967, 217p.

**13**
*Reynosa, Mexico and the McAllen-Pharr-Edinburg SMSA: a Statistical Abstract*. McAllen, TX, McAllen Chamber of Commerce, 1967, 46p.

**14**
Wionczek, Miguel S.
*El Nacionalismo Mexicano y la Inversión Extranjera*. México, Siglo 21 Editores, 1967, 314p.

**15**
Campos, Salas, O.
"El Desarrollo Industrial en 1966." México, *Revista de Economía* (30: 4), April 1967, pp. 98-105.

**16**
Bohrisch, A., & König, W.
"Die Haltung Mexikos zu Ausländischen Direktinvestitionen." Berlin, *Schmöllers Jahrbuch* (87: 5), 1967, pp. 567-606.

**17**
Ericson, Anna-Stina L.
"Economic Development in the Mexican Border Areas." *Labor Developments Abroad* (U.S. Dept. of Labor) (12: 6), June 1967, pp. 1-8.

**18**
Dillman, C. D.
"Urban Growth Along Mexico's Border and the Mexican National Border Program." *Journal of Developing Areas* (4: 4), July 1967, pp. 487-508.

**19**
"Mexico Offers Opportunities for Joint Venture Capital." *Business Abroad* 92, July 10, 1967, pp. 33-35.

**20**

"Investment Opportunities in Mexican Industrial Exports Cited in Study." *International Commerce* 73, September 25, 1967, p. 26.

**21**

"Mexico's Success Story." *U.S. News & World Report* 63, October 2, 1967, pp. 53-56.

**22**

"Mexican Border Towns Lure Gringo Industry." *Business Week* December 2, 1967, pp. 120-122.

**23**

Miller, S.
"Siren Call Heard South of the Border." *Electronic News* 12, December 4, 1967, p. 1.

**24**

"Wetbacks in Reverse: why U.S. Firms Cross the Border into Mexico." *Business Abroad* 92, December 11, 1967, pp. 20-21.

*1968*

**25**

Dillman, C. D.
*The Functions of Brownsville, Texas, and Matamoros, Tamaulipas; Twin Cities of the Lower Rio Grande.* Ann Arbor, MI, 1968, 215p. (Ph.D. Dissertation, University of Michigan)

**26**

Enjalbert, H.
*Algunas Ideas Sobre Regulación Geográfica Economica en México: Conferencias.* México, Comisión Nacional de los Salarios Mínimos, 1968, 128p.

**27**

Freithaler, W. O.
*Mexico's Foreign Trade and Economic Development.* New York, Praeger, 1968, 160p.

**28**

Strassman, W. P.
*Technological Change and Economic Development; the Manufacturing Experience of Mexico and Puerto Rico.* Ithaca, NY, Cornell University Press, 1968, 353p.

**29**

Whitt, John D.
*Profit Planning and Control in Foreign Operations With Specific Application to Mexican Subsidiaries of U.S. Parent Firms.* University, MS, 1968, 276p. (Ph.D. Dissertation, University of Mississippi)

**30**

Mendoza Berrueto, E.
"Regional Implications of Mexico's Economic Growth." Hamburg, Germany, *Weltwirtschaftliches Archiv* (101: 1), 1968, pp. 87-123.

**31**

Price, J. A.
"Tijuana: a Study of Symbiosis." *New Mexico Quarterly* (38: 3), 1968, pp. 8-18.

**32**

Villareal Cárdenas, Rodolfo
"Industrialization of Mexico's Northern Border and the United States Investor." *Arizona Review* (17: 1), January 1968, pp. 6-9.

**33**

Christman, John H.
"Border Industries Foster New Jobs, More Exports." Mexico, *Mexican American Review* (36: 2), February 1968, pp. 9-15.

**34**

Urquidi, V.
"An Overview of Mexican Economic Development." Hamburg, *Weltwirtschaftliches Archiv* (100: 2), 1968, pp. 2-20.

**35**
Taylor, B. J., & Bond, M. E.
"Mexican Border Industrialization." *Michigan State University Business Topics* 16, Spring 1968, pp. 33-45.

**36**
"Los Californios 'Descubren' un Mercado Mexicano." México, *Comercio Exterior* (18: 4), April 1968, pp. 318-319.

**37**
Zamora Millán, F.
"La Intervención del Estado y el Desarrollo Económico." México, *Revista de Desarrollo Económico* (31: 4), April 1968, pp. 106-118.

**38**
Keenan, Joseph et al.
*United States-Mexico Border Problems*. Report to the Subcommittee on International Relations of the AFL-CIO Executive Council, May 14, 1968. Washington, AFL-CIO, 1968.

**39**
Rostow, W. W.
"U.S.-Mexico Border Commission Holds Second Plenary Session; Remarks with Dept. Announcement, April 30, May 1, 1968." *U.S. Dept. of State Bulletin* 58, May 27, 1968, pp. 692-693.

**40**
"Things Look up for Mexico as U.S. Crosses the Border." *U.S. News & World Report* 65, July 1, 1968, pp. 78-79.

**41**
Jackson, R. S., Jr.
"The Border Industrialization Program of Northern Mexico." Paper presented at Seminar in Latin American Commercial Law, University of Texas at Austin, Fall 1968.

**42**
Samuelson, Paul A.
"Les Investissements Directs Américains dans une Économie Engagée dans le Développement: le cas du Méxique." Paris, *Revue de Science Financière* (60: 4), October-December 1968, pp. 896-954.

**43**
García Reynoso, P.
"La Política Mexicana de Fomento Industrial." México, *Revista de Economía* (31: 11), November 1968, pp. 337-343.

*1969*

**44**
Farias Negrete, Jorge
*Industrialization Program for the Mexican Northern Border.* México, Ed. Jus, 1969, 75p.

**45**
*General Information on Mexico's Border Industrialization Program for U.S. Manufacturers at Reynosa, Tamp., Mexico.* McAllen, TX, McAllen Chamber of Commerce, 1969, 30p.

**46**
*Survey on Border Development Programs.* Report of the Subcommittee on Mexican Border and Regional Development Problems of the International Trade and Investment Committee. México, American Chamber of Commerce of Mexico, 1969.

**47**
Texas. University. Institute of Latin American Studies
*Basic Industries in Texas and Northern Mexico.* Conference sponsored by the Institute of Latin American Studies of the University of Texas, June 9-11, 1949. New York, Greenwood Press, 1969, 193p.

**48**
U.S. House of Representatives
*United States-Mexico Commission for Border Development and*

*Friendship*. Report 91-556, to Accompany House-Senate Joint Resolution 894 (91st Congress, first session). Washington, GPO, 1969.

**49**

Valencia, Nestor A.
*Twentieth Century Urbanization in Latin America and a Case Study of Ciudad Juarez*. El Paso: 1969. (Master's Thesis, University of Texas at El Paso)

**50**

Mendoza Berrueto, E.
"Implicaciones Regionales del Desarrollo Económico de México." México, *Demografía y Economía* (3: 1), 1969, pp. 25-63.

**51**

Walker, Harold O., Jr.
"Border Industries With a Mexican Accent." *Columbia Journal of World Business*, January/February 1969, pp. 25-32.

**52**

"Phosphoric Experts on way From Mexico." *Oil, Paint & Drug Reporter* 195, January 13, 1969, p. 3.

**53**

James, Dilmus D.
"An Economic Appraisal of the Mexican Border Industrialization Program." Paper presented at Meeting of the Western Regional Science Association, Newport Beach, CA, February 1969.

**54**

"Developments in Mexican Border Industrialization." *Texas International Law Forum* 5, Spring 1969, p. 164.

**55**

Giblin, P. M.
"Developments in Mexican Border Industrialization." *Texas International Law Forum* 5, Spring 1969, pp. 164-175.

**56**
Treviño, Julio B.
"Border Assembly Operations." México, *Mexican-American Review* 37, April 1969, pp. 31-33.

**57**
Dillman, C. D.
"Brownsville: Border Port for Mexico and the United States." *Professional Geographer* 21, May 1969, pp. 178-183.

**58**
Lopez, D.
"Low Wage Lures South of the Border." *American Federationist* 76, June 1969, pp. 1-7.

**59**
"Borderline Industry; Effect of Industrialization Program." *Newsweek* 73, June 23, 1969, p. 82.

**60**
Schooler, R. D., & Gonzalez-Arce, J.
"Attitudes of Residents Toward U.S.-Mexico Border Industrialization." *Michigan State University Business Topics* 17, Summer 1969, pp. 58-64.

**61**
Stoddard, Elwyn R.
"The United States-Mexico Border as a Research Laboratory." *Journal of Inter-American Studies* 11, July 1969, pp. 477-488.

**62**
"Jumping Market Below the Border." *Business Week*, July 12, 1969, pp. 120-121.

**63**
"The Mexican Export Industries." London, *Bank of London & South America* (3: 34), October 1969, pp. 623-626.

**64**
"Ofensiva Sindical Norteamericana Contra las Industrias Fronter-izas." México, *Comercio Exterior* (19: 10), October 1969, p. 774.

**65**
Sunkel, Osvaldo
"National Development Policy and External Dependence in Latin America." London, *Journal of Development Studies* (6: 1), October 1969, pp. 23-48.

**66**
"Régimen Legal y de Promoción de las Industrias Fronterizas." México, *Comercio Exterior* (19: 11), November 1969, pp. 865-866.

**67**
Alcalá Quintero, F.
"Desarrollo Regional Fronterizo." México, *Comercio Exterior* 19, December 1969, pp. 960-964.

**68**
"Desarrollo Regional: los Problemas de la Región Fronteriza Norte." México, *Comercio Exterior* (19: 12), December 1969, pp. 973-974.

**69**
Dillman, C. D.
"Border Town Symbiosis Along the Lower Rio Grande as Ex-emplified by the Twin Cities, Brownsville (Texas) and Matamo-ros (Tamaulipas)." México, *Revista Geográfica* 71, December 1969, pp. 93-113.

*1970*

**70**
Link, M.
*Die Ursachen des Industriellen Aufstiegs Mexikos*. Zürich, Switzerland, Orell Füssli Verlag, 1970, 229p.

**71**

*Selected Reprints of Articles on Mexico's Border Industrial Program.* McAllen, TX, McAllen Chamber of Commerce, 197—, 20p.

**72**

"Desarrollo Regional: se Confirma la Realización de Audiencias Sobre las Industrias Fronterizas." México, *Comercio Exterior* (20: 1), January 1970, p. 33.

**73**

Luiselli Fernandez, C.
"Los Estímulos Fiscales y Financieros a la Industrialización." México, *Investigación Económica* (30: 117), January-March 1970, pp. 131-152.

**74**

Dillman, C. D.
"Commuter Workers and Free Zone Industry Along the U.S. Mexico Border." (In: Association of *American Geographers. Proceedings*, 2. Washington, 1970, pp. 48-51).

**75**

Dillman, C. D.
"Transformation of the Lower Rio Grande of Texas and Tamaulipas." *Ecumene* (2: 2), 1970, pp. 3-11.

**76**

Faesler, J.
"La Industria Mexicana y los Mercados Internacionales." México, *Comercio Exterior* 20, February 1970, pp. 140-144.

**77**

"Border Plants Team U.S. Know-how, Mexican Labor." *Industry Week* 166, February 16, 1970, pp. 10-11.

**78**

Morelos, J. B., & Lerner, S.
"Proyecciones de la Población Total y de la Población Activa de

México por Regiones, 1960-1985.'' México, *Demografía y Economía* (4: 3), 1970, pp. 349-363.

**79**
Tabah, L.
''Mesure de la Migration Interne au Moyen des Recensements. Application au Méxique.'' Paris, *Population* (25: 2), March-April 1970, pp. 303-346.

**80**
''Desarrollo Regional: PRONAF—Respuesta al Desafío Comercial Fronterizo.'' México, *Comercio Exterior* (20: 4), April 1970, pp. 301-302.

**81**
Hunt, Lacy
''Desarrollo Indutrial en la Frontera Mexicana.'' México, *Comercio Exterior* (20: 4), April 1970, pp. 304-309.

**82**
Ericson, Anna-Stina L.
''An Analysis of Mexico's Border Industrialization Program.'' *Monthly Labor Review* (93: 5), May 1970, pp. 33-40.

**83**
''Levy on Assemblies for U.S. Clouds Mexico Job Picture.'' *Electronic News* 15, May 4, 1970, p. 33.

**84**
''Desarrollo Regional: Empresas Maquiladoras Fronterizas—Facilidades Aduaneras y Debate Sobre su Futuro.'' México, *Comercio Exterior* (20: 6), June 1970, p. 453.

**85**
Dillman, C. D.
''Urban Growth Along Mexico's Northern Border and the Mexican National Border Program.'' *Journal of Developing Areas* 4, July 1970, pp. 487-507.

**86**

"Many Faces of Industrial Mexico." *Modern Manufacturing* 3, July 1970, pp. 42-47.

**87**

"Clairol de Mexico Launches new Line." *Advertising Age* 41, August 10, 1970, p. 31.

**88**

"Mexico." *Business Week*, August 16, 1976, pp. 19-41.

**89**

"Desarrollo Regional: Maquiladras y Comercio Fronterizo — se Despeja el Panorama." México, *Comercio Exterior* (20: 9), September 1970, pp. 746-747.

**90**

Dillman, C. D.
"Recent Developments in Mexico's National Border Program." *Professional Geographer* 22, September 1970, pp. 243-247.

**91**

"Cars: Spares From Mexico." *The Economist* 236, September 5, 1970, p. 86.

**92**

Wionczek, Miguel S.
"La Inversión Extranjera Privada en México: Problemas y Perspectivas." México, *Comercio Exterior* 20, October 1970, pp. 816-824.

*1971*

**93**

Hansen, R. D.
*Mexican Economic Development; the Roots of Rapid Growth.* Washington, National Planning Association, 1971, 150p.

**94**

Hansen, R. D.
*The Politics of Mexican Development*. Baltimore, Johns Hopkins University Press, 1971, 267p.

**95**

Katz, Bernard S.
*Mexican Import Policy and Industrialization, 1929-1965*. Storrs, CT, 1971, 220. (Ph.D. Dissertation, University of Connecticut)

**96**

Ladman, J., & Poulson, M. O.
*Economic Impact of the Mexican Border Industrialization Program: Agua Prieta, Sonora*. Tempe, AZ, Center for Latin American Studies, Arizona State University, 1971. (Publication #10)

**97**

May, Herbert K., & Fernandez Arena, José A.
*The Impact of Foreign Investment in Mexico*. Washington, National Chamber Foundation, 1971, 92p.

**98**

México. Secretaría de Industria y Comercio
*Programa de Industralización de la Frontera Norte de México*. México, 1971, 40p.

**99**

Ramos Garza, Oscar
*México ante la Inversión Extranjera; Legislación Politica y Prácticas*. México, 1971, 306p.

**100**

Wright, Harry K.
*Foreign Enterprise in Mexico; Laws and Policies*. Chapel Hill, University of North Carolina Press, 1971, 425p.

**101**

Morelos, J. B.
"El Desarrollo Económico y los Recursos Humanos en México:

un Esquema Conceptual." México, *Demografía y Economía* (5: 2), 1971, pp. 131-144.

**102**

Bolin, Richard L.
"Border Industries: A Rebuttal." México, *Mexican-American Review* (39: 3), March 1971, pp. 21, 23.

**103**

"Fragmentos del Informe de la Comisión de Aranceles de Estados Unidos Sobre las Industrias Maquiladoras de Exportación." México, *Comercio Exterior* (21: 4), April 1971, pp. 292-308.

**104**

"Las Industrias Maquiladoras de Exportación." México, *Comercio Exterior* (21: 4), April 1971, pp. 274-276.

**105**

Mujica, Emilio M.
"Hacia una Política Realista de Desarrollo Fronterizo." México, *Comercio Exterior* (21: 4), April 1971, pp. 318-321.

**106**

"Nuevo Reglamento para las Industrias Maquiladoras de Exportación." México, *Comercio Exterior* (21: 4), April 1971, pp. 290-291.

**107**

Tansik, David A., & Tapia S., Humberto
"Los Problemas de las 'Plantas Gemelas' en la Frontera Mexicana." México, *Comercio Exterior* (21: 4), April 1971, pp. 331-335.

**108**

Caso, A. "El Empleo como Objetivo del Desarrollo." México, *Trimestre Económico* (20: 150), April-June 1971, pp. 259-274.

**109**

Flores de la Peña, H.
"México: el Marco Económico de la Política de Industrializa-

ción. Ensayo en Honor de Michal Kalecki." México, *Trimestre Económico* (38: 150), April-June 1971, pp. 323-333.

**110**
"Desarrollo Regional: Impulso al Desarrollo de la Zona Fronteriza Norte." Mexico, *Comercio Exterior* (21: 5), May 1971, pp. 387-389.

**111**
"Desarrollo Regional: Prórroga del Tratamiento Fiscal Preferencial a la Zona Fronteriza." México, *Comercio Exterior* (21: 7), July 1971, p. 588.

**112**
Kent, J. E.
"The Role of Industrial Parks in the Twin Plant Concept." *Industrial Development* 140, July 1971, pp. 6-8.

**113**
Steiner, H. M.
"Twin Plants Sprout Along U.S.-Mexican Border." *Industrial Development* 140, July 1971, pp. 2-5.

**114**
"AFL-CIO to U.S. Government: Stop Encouraging Runaways." *The Machinist* 26, July 15, 1971.

**114-A**
Mora Ortiz, Gonzalo
"El Desarrollo Económico Regional Como Base para el Fomento y Diversificación de las Exportaciones." México: *Comercio Exterior* 21, September 1971, pp. 757-759.

**114-B**
Vaitsos, Constantine V.
"Opciones Estratégicas en la Comercialización de Tecnología: el Punto de Vista de los Países en Desarrollo." Mexico: *Comercio Exterior* 21, September 1971, pp. 806-815.

**114-C**
Wionczek, Miguel S.
"Los Problemas de la Transferencia de Tecnología en un Marco de Industrialización Accelerada." México: *Comercio Exterior* 21, September 1971, pp. 782-794.

**115**
"Cel Mex Maps 10-Year Buildup." *Chemical Week* 109, September 15, 1971, p. 23.

**116**
Budd, Jim
"PRONAF's First Decade." Mexico, *Mexican-American Review* (39: 10), October 1971, pp. 12-13, 15.

**117**
Trejo Reyes, S.
"Un Modelo de Política Económica: Promoción de Exportanciones y Crecimiento Óptimo de la Economía." México, *Trimestre Económico* (38: 152), October-December 1971, pp. 1041-1067.

**118**
Hoefler, D. C.
"Mexico." *Electronic News* 16, October 4, 1971, pp. 4-5.

**119**
"Corporaciones Transnacionales y Empresas Multinacionales." México, *Comercio Exterior* 21, November 1971, pp. 978-982.

**119-A**
"Decreto que Declara de Utilidad Nacional el Establecimiento y Ampliación de Empresas para Impulsar el Desarrollo Regional: Texto del Decreto Presidencial Expedido el 23 de Noviembre de 1971." Mexico: *Mercado de Valores 31*, November 29, 1971, p. 905.

## *1972*

**120**

James, Dilmus D.

"The Mexican Border Industrialization Program and the Economic Development of Northern Mexico." Paper presented at Seminar for Visiting Mexican Economists, University of Arizona, Tucson, AZ, 1972.

**121**

Jeanjean, L., & Revel-Mouroz, J.

*Villes de la Frontière Méxique-États-Unis; Population et Économie de Deux Villes Jumelles: Ciudad Jarez—El Paso.* Paris, Centre National de la Recherche Scientifique, 1972, 85p.

**122**

*Memoria del Coloquio Sobre Planificación Regional.* México, Instituto de Geografía, Universidad Nacional Autónoma de México, 1972, 296p.

**123**

Mexico. Laws, statutes, etc.

*Reglamento del Párrafo Tercero del Artículo 321 del Código Aduanero de los Estados Unidos Mexicanos para el Fomento de la Industria Maquiladora.* México, Secretaría de Gobernación, 1972.

**124**

Taylor, J. R.

*Twin Plants and the Border Industrialization Program.* (Volume 4: Needs Analysis of the Port of Anapra Development Program). Las Cruces, NM: Center for Business Services, New Mexico State University, 1972.

**125**

Vetterli, R. R.

*The Impact of the Multinational Corporation on the Power Structure of Mexico and a Mexican Border Community.* Riverside,

CA, 1972, 479p. (Ph.D. Dissertation, University of California, Riverside).

**125-A**
Vega-Centeno, Máximo
"Mecanismos de Difusión del Conocimiento y Elección de Tecnología." México: *Comercio Exterior* 22, January 1972, pp. 61-66.

**126**
"A Business Boomlet on Mexico's Border." *Business Week*, January 22, 1972, pp. 36-38.

**127**
"Big Deal at the Border." *Newsweek* 79, January 27, 1972, pp. 59-60.

**128**
"Allen Bradley Planning Mexican Resistor Facility." *Electronic News* 17, January 31, 1972, p. 26.

**129**
Razo Oliva, J. D.
"Mexico, Desarrollo con Desempleo Creciente." México, *Problemas del Desarrollo* (3: 10), February-April 1972, pp. 115-123.

**130**
Aguilar Alvarez, I., & Lamadrid Ibarra, A.
"Desarrollo Socioeconómico Comparativo de las Entidades del País, 1940-1970." México, *Comercio Exterior de México* (22: 3), March 1972, pp. 255-265.

**131**
Taylor, J. R.
"Industrialization of the Mexican Border Region." *New Mexico Business* 26, March 1972, pp. 3-9.

**132**
"Spread of U.S. Plants to Mexico Brings a Boom and Complaints." *U.S. News & World Report* 72, March 27, 1972, pp. 57-59.

**133**
Arellano Rincón, S.
"Política de Desarrollo Industrial." México, *Pensamiento Político* (9: 36), April 1972, pp. 457-472.

**134**
"330 Fábricas en 6 Años Gracias al Plan Fronterizo Mexicano." México, *Progresso* (5: 3), April 1972, pp. 29-31.

**135**
Bassols Batalla, A.
"Mexico: Regiones Económicas y Regiones Agrícolas." México, *Problemas del Desarrollo* (3: 11), May-July 1972, pp. 23-52.

**136**
Gutierrez Treviño, E.
"Transformación de la Zona Fronteriza Norte-Mexicana." México, *Mercado de Valores* 32, May 22, 1972, pp. 507-509.

**137**
Calvert, Peter
"Regional Development in Mexico." London, *Bank of London & South America Review* (6: 66), June 1972, pp. 304-310.

**138**
Evans, John S.
"Mexican Border Development and its Impact Upon the United States." *Southeastern Latinamericanist* 16, June 1972, pp. 4-10.

**139**
"Desarrollo Regional: Fomento Económico en la Frontera Norte e Industrias Maquiladoras." México, *Comercio Exterior* (22: 7), July 1972, pp. 607-608.

**140**
Sanchez Herrero, S.
"Nueva Etapa de las Relaciones Económicas." México, *Pensamiento Político* (10: 39), July 1972, pp. 337-344.

**141**
Ramíez Rancaño, M., & Galicia, S. R.
"La Penetración Imperialista en México." México, *Problemas del Desarrollo* (3: 12), August-December 1972, pp. 101-138.

**141-A**
Aguilar, C., Juan J.
"Camino Inexplorado: Adaptación de Tecnología." Mexico: *Transformación* 12, August 1972, pp. 4-10.

**141-B**
*Mercado de Valores*. Mexico: August 21, 1972— (special issue covering industrial planning of the Border region of Northern Mexico).

**142**
"Industrial Planning—U.S.-Mexican Border." México, *Mercado de Valores*, August 21, 1972 (entire issue).

**143**
Martínez Dominguez, Guillermo
"Participación de Nacional Financiera en el Desarrollo de la Frontera Norte del País." México, *El Mercado de Valores* (32: 34), August 21, 1972, pp. 849, 851-853.

**144**
Lavell, A. M.
"Regional Industrialization in Mexico: Some Policy Considerations." Oxford, England, *Regional Studies* (6: 3), September 1972, pp. 343-362.

**145**
Camejo, A.
"Runaway Industries Exploit Mexico." New York, *Militant* (36: 19), September 19, 1972, p. 17.

**146**
Barkin, David
  "A Mexican Case Study: the Demographic Aspect of Regional Development." *Growth & Change* (3: 4), October 1972, pp. 15-22.

**147**
Campillo Sainz, J.
  "Las Inversiones Extranjeras en México." México, *Mercado de Valores* 32, October 16, 1972, pp. 1091-1097.

**148**
"Mexican Attitude Toward U.S. Border Firms Noted." *Los Angeles Times*, November 12, 1972, section 1, p. 1, column 6.

**149**
Fernandez, Raúl A.
  "The Border Industrial Program on the United States-Mexico Border." *Review of Radical Political Economy* (5: 1), 1973, pp. 37-52.

*1973*

**149-A**
Carrillo Aronte, Ricardo
  *Ensayo Analítico Metodológico de Planificación Interregional en México*. México: Fondo de Cultura Economica, 1973, 244p.

**150**
Gilpin, Robert
  *The Multinational Corporation and the National Interest*. Report to the Senate Committee on Labor and Public Welfare, Washington, DC, U.S. Government Printing Office, 1973, 85p. (At head of title: 93d Congress. 1st session. Committee print.)

**151**
Moore, Russell M.
  *The Role of U.S. Companies in the Expansion of Mexico's Non-Traditional Exports*. Paper presented at the Conference on Economic Relations Between Mexico and the United States, Univer-

sity of Texas, 1973. Austin, University of Texas at Austin, Institute of Latin American Studies, 1973, 14p.

**152**
Pomeroy, J. P., & Nash, R. H.
*Investing in Mexico*. Houston, Universal Services Association, 1973, 168p.

**153**
Price, J. A.
*Tijuana: Urbanization in a Border Culture*. Notre Dame, IN, University of Notre Dame Press, 1973, 195p.

**154**
Rivas Sosa, E.
*Función de las Industrias Maquiladoras en la Promoción de Polos de Desarrollo Industria*. México: Universidad Nacional Autónoma de México, Escuela Nacional de Economía, 1973. (Professional thesis).

**155**
Sepúlveda Amor, Bernardo, & Chumacero, Antonio
*La Inversión Extranjera en México*. México, Fondo de Cultura Económica, 1973, 262p. (Note: this article contains a list of 170 U.S. firms and their subsidiaries in Mexico.)

**156**
Trejo Reyes, S.
*Industrialización y Empleo en México*. México, Fondo de Cultura Económica, 1973, 198p.

**157**
Turner, Louis
*Multinational Corporations and the Third World*. New York, Hill & Wang, 1973, 294p.

**158**
Guzmán Ferrer, M. L. et al.
"Mexico: Desarrollo de las Distintas Entidades Territoriales del

País, 1940-1970.'' Geneva, Switzerland, *Mondes en Développement* 1, 1973, pp. 165-193.

**159**
Soto Mora, Consuelo
"Problemas Socioeconómicos de la Frontera Norte de México."
México, *Anuario de Geografía* 13, 1973, pp. 175-210.

**160**
Wenzens, G.
"Wirtschaftliche Veränderungen in der Comarca Lagunera (Nord-Mexiko), unter Besonderer Berücksichtigung der Industrialisierung." Brunswick, Federal Republic of Germany, *Geographische Rundschau* 25, January 1973, pp. 12-16.

**161**
Revel-Mouroz, J.
"L'Industrialisation de la Frontière Méxique-États Unis par les Maquiladoras." Paris, *Cahiers des Amériques Latines* 7, January-June 1973, pp. 202-221.

**162**
Franser, J.
"South of the Border: a Little Latitude." *Electronic News* 18, January 8, 1973, pp. 4-5.

**163**
Campillo Sainz, J.
"Tecnología y Capital Extranjero en Términos Convenientes a la Economía Nacional." México, *Mercado de Valores* 33, January 29, 1973, p. 129.

**164**
"Desarrollo Regional: IV Reunión de Trabajo para el Desarrollo Fronterizo." México, *Comercio Exterior* (23: 3), March 1973, pp. 217-219.

**165**

Helleiner, G. K.

"Manufactured Exports from Less Developed Countries and Multinational Firms." *Economics Journal* 83, March 1973, pp. 21-47.

**166**

Fernandez, R. A.

"The Border Industrialization Program on the U.S.-Mexican Border." Ann Arbor, *Review of Radical Political Economics* (5: 1), Spring 1973, pp. 37-52.

**167**

Berni, G.

"Border Industry: the Case of Ciudad Juarez, Chihuahua." Paper presented at Conference sponsored by the Institute of Latin American Studies, University of Texas at Austin, April 1973.

**168**

Erickson, Rosemary J.

*Social Profiles of San Diego*. La Jolla, CA, Western Behavioral Sciences Institute, 1973-74, 3v.

**169**

Fouts, Susan (Carey)

"Mexican Border Industrialization: an Analogy and a Comment." Paper presented at Conference sponsored by the Institute of Latin American Studies, University of Texas at Austin, April 1973.

**170**

Langer, Frédéric

"Les Compagnies Américaines s'Emparent de la Frontière Méxicaine." Paris, *Croissance des Jeunes Nations* 134, April 1973, pp. 9-13.

**171**

Moran, T. H.

"Foreign Investment as an 'Institutional Necessity' for U.S.

Corporate Capitalism: the Search for a Radical Model." *World Politics* (25: 3), April 1973, p. 369.

**172**
Murguía Rosette, J. A.
*Foreign Investment as a Factor in Development*. Paper presented at Conference of the Institute of Latin American Studies, University of Texas at Austin, April 1973.

**173**
Taylor, J. R.
"Industrialization of the Mexican Border Region." *New Mexico Business* 26, March 1973, pp. 3-9.

**174**
Villalobos Calderón, L.
"On the Importance of the Assembly Industries to the Mexican Economy." Paper presented at Conference of the Institute of Latin American Studies, University of Texas at Austin, April 1973.

**175**
Villalobos Calderón, L.
"La Industria Maquiladora Extranjera en México: mal Necesario de una Sociedad Subdesarrollada." Mexico, *Relaciones Internacionales* (1: 1), April-June 1973, pp. 5-21.

**176**
Bosse, C.
"Noagles, Sonora: Prosperity From Piccolos, Paper Dresses, Printed Circuits." *Industrial Development* 142, May 1973, pp. 18-23.

**177**
Rostro, F.
"Anatomía de una Política." México, *Transformación* 13, May 1973, pp. 4-6.

**178**

Bueno Zirión, Gerardo
"La Transferencia de Tecnología en México." México: *Mercado de Valores* 33, July 16, 1973, pp. 989-993. (speech)

**179**

Cone, C. A.
"Perceptions of Occupations in a Newly Industrializing Region of Mexico." *Human Organization* 32, Summer 1973, pp. 143-151.

**180**

"Desarrollo Regional: V Reunión de Trabajo Sobre Desarrolo Fronterizo." México, *Comercio Exterior* (23: 7), July 1973, pp. 618-619.

**181**

Hendon, Donald W.
"The Border Industrialization Program." *Mexican American Review* (41: 7), July 1973, pp. 15-17, 19.

**182**

"La Frontera sur de los Estados Unidos de Norteamérica: Perfil Socioeconómico." México, *Mercado de Valores* 33, July 9, 1973, pp. 959-963.

**183**

Bolin, Richard L.
"Border Industry Facts for 1973." *Mexican American Review* (41: 9), September 1973, pp. 14-15, 17, 19, 21, 23.

**184**

Syrquin, M.
"Efficient Input Frontiers for the Manufacturing Sector in Mexico, 1965-1980." *International Economic Review* (14: 3), October 1973, pp. 567-675.

**185**
"La Industria Maquiladora Fronteriza." México, *El Mercado de Valores* (33: 44), October 29, 1973, pp. 1506-1508.

**185-A**
Fernandez, R. A.
"Economy and Change on the United States-Mexico Border." Paper presented to Meeting of the Association for the Study of North American Integration, New York, NY, December 1973.

**186**
"Bowmar Instruments to Build Third Assembly Plant in Mexico." *Los Angeles Times*, December 7, 1973, section 3, p. 19, column 1.

**186-A**
"Document Méxique." Paris: *Moniteur du Commerce International* (new series), December 17, 1973, p. 11.

**187**
"Increase in Mexican Taxes Viewed." *Los Angeles Times*, December 22, 1973, section 1, p. 10, column 5.

### 1974

**188**
Barnet, Richard J., & Müller, Ronald E.
*Global Reach: the Power of Multinational Corporations*. New York: Simon & Schuster, 1974, 508p.

**189**
Evans, John S., & James, Dilmus D.
"The Industrialization of the Northern Mexico Border Region: Past, Present and Future." Revision of paper presented to Meeting of the Southwestern Economics Association, Dallas, TX, 1974.

**189-A**
Müller-Ohlsen, Lotte
*Importsubstitution and Exportdiversifizierung im Industriali-*

*sierungsprozess Mexikos: Strategien, Ergebnisse, Perspektiven.* Kiel, Germany: Universität Kiel, Instituut für Weltwirtschaft, 1974, 284p.

**190**

Gildersleeve, C. R.
"Ambos Nogales and Douglas-Agua Prieta: Comparisons of Two Paired Cities on the United States-Mexico Border." Paper presented at the Meeting of the Association of American Geographers, Seattle, WA, April 1974.

**191**

Moxon, R. W.
*Offshore Production in the Less-Developed Countries: a Case Study of Multinationals in the Electronics Industry* (Bulletin nos. 98-99). New York: New York University, Graduate School of Business Administration, Institute of Finance, July 1974.

**192**

Palmore, Glenn L. et al.
*The Ciudad Juarez Plan for Comprehensive Socio-Economic Development: a Model for Northern Mexico Border Cities.* El Paso: University of Texas at El Paso, Bureau of Business & Economic Research, 1974.

**193**

Sepúlveda Amor, Bernardo et al.
*Las Empresas Transnacionales en México.* México, Colegio de México, 1974, 167p.

**194**

United States. Information Agency. Office of Research
*Mexican Elite Attitudes Toward Foreign Investment.* Washington, 1974, 27p.

**195**

Haight, G. W. et al.
"Should Investment Capital Stay Home? A Mexico-United States Dialogue." *The American Journal of International Law Proceedings* 68, 1974, pp. 58-75.

**196**

"Transnacionales y Mano de Obra: el Caso de las Maquiladoras de la Frontera Norte de México." México, *Comunicaciones* (Centro Nacional de Comunicación Social), 1974.

**197**

Watanabe, S.
  "Constraints on Labor-Intensive Export Industries in Mexico." Geneva, Switzerland, *International Labour Review* 109, January 1974, pp. 23-45.

**198**

"Doce Mil Obreras en Huelga en Nuevo Laredo." México, *Punto Crítico* (25/26), February-March 1974, top half of pages.

**199**

"Las Maquiladoras Como Explotación Neocolonial." México, *Punto Crítico* (25/26), February-March 1974, lower half of pages.

**200**

Molina Ruibal, A.
  "La Estrategia Mexicana de Desarrollo: un Tercer Camino." México, *Pensamiento Político* (15: 59), March 1974, pp. 307-320.

**201**

"Boom South of the Border Gets Bigger." *Industry Week* 180, March 4, 1974, pp. 32-33.

**202**

"Mexico's Border Industrial Program" (In: *Comment* section, *Denver Journal of International Law & Policy* 4, Spring 1974, pp. 1-109).

**203**

Cohn, J. W.
  "Mexico Rules out Nationalization of In-Bond Plants." *Electronic News* 19, March 25, 1974, p. 51.

**204**
Dillman, C. D.
"Assembly Plants in Mexico's Northern Border Cities and the Border Industrialization Program." Paper presented to Association of American Geographers Conference, Seattle, Washington, April 1974.

**205**
Jopling, C. R.
"Women's Work: a Mexican Case Study of Low Status as a Tactical Advantage." *Ethnology* 13, April 1974, pp. 187-195.

**206**
Ayer, H. W., & Layton, M. R.
"The Border Industry Program and the Impacts of Expenditures by Mexican Border Industry Employees on a U.S. Border Community: an Empirical Study of Nogales, Arizona." *Annals of Regional Science* 8, June 1974, pp. 105-117.

**207**
Bolin, Richard L.
"Border Industry Facts: the First Billion-Dollar Year." Mexico, *Mexican American Review* (42: 6), June 1974, pp. 18-19.

**208**
"Desarrollo Regional: VI Reunión Nacional para el Desarrollo Fronterizo." México, *Comercio Exterior* (24: 7), July 1974, pp. 683, 686-688.

**209**
Vallejo Hinojosa, M.
"Inversión Extranjera, Independencia y Desarrollo." México, *Pensamiento Político* 16, July 1974, pp. 327-336.

**210**
Syrquin, M.
"Las Fronteras de Eficiencia de los Insumos en el Sector Manufacturero de México, 1965-1980." México, *Trimestre Económico* (41: 163), July-September 1974, pp. 625-647.

**211**
Villar, S. I. del
"La Necesidad de Regular la Inversión Extranjera. Criterios para su Evaluación." México, *Foro Internacional* (15: 1), July-September 1974, pp. 13-52.

**212**
Cable, V.
"The Role of Foreign Investment." London, *Bank of London & South America* (92: 8), August 1974, pp. 457-466.

**213**
"In-Bond Industry Holds Dialogue." Mexico, *Mexican American Review* (42: 8), August 1974, p. 40.

**214**
Loehr, W., & Bulson, M. E.
"The Mexican Border Industrialization Program." *Arizona Business* 21, October 1974, pp. 11-16.

**215**
"Maquiladroas: the Road Ahead." Mexico, *Mexican American Review* (42: 11), November 1974, pp. 4-7, 9, 11, 13.

**216**
Villareal Cárdenas, Rodolfo
"El Desequilibrio Externo en el Crecimiento Económico de México." México, *Trimestre Económico* (41: 164), October-December 1974, pp. 775-810.

*1975*

**217**
Aguilera Gomez, Manuel
*La Desnacionalización de la Economía Mexicana.* México, Fondo de Cultural Económica, 1975, 155p.

**218**
Bustamante, Jorge A.
"El Programa Fronterizo de Maquiladoras: Observaciones para

una Evaluación." México: *Foro Internacional* (16: 2), 1975, pp. 183-204.

**219**
Chapoy Bonifaz, Alma de María
"Empresas Maquiladoras (In her, *Empresas Multinacionales*, México, Ediciones El Caballito, 1975, pp. 219-229).

**220**
Gilpin, Robert
*U.S. Power and the Multinational Corporation; the Political Economy of Foreign Direct Investment*. New York, Basic Books, 1975, 291p.

**221**
Newfarmer, Richard S., & Mueller, Willard F.
*Multinational Corporations in Brazil and Mexico: Structural Sources of Economic and non-Economic Power*. Report to the Subcommittee on Multinational Corporations of the Committee on Foreign Relations, U.S. Senate. Washington, GPO, 1975, 212p. (94th Congress, 1st Session)

**222**
Urquidi, Victor L., & Mendez Villareal, Sofia
"Importancia Económica de la Zona Fronteriza del Norte de México." México: *Foro Internacional* (16: 2), 1975, pp. 149-174.

**222-A**
Unikel, Luis
"Políticas de Desarrollo Regional en México." México: *Demografía y Economía* (11: 2), 1975, pp. 143-181.

**223**
Waarts, A.
*The Inter-Regional Planning Model for Mexico: the Data Base*. Rotterdam, Center for Development Planning, Erasmus University, 1975, 68p.

**224**

Garcia, B.

"La participación de la Población en la Actividad Económica."
México, *Demografía y Economía* (9: 1), 1975, pp. 1-31.

**225**

Barr, Lorna

"NAWAPA: a Continental Development Scheme for North
America." *Geography* (60: 2), 1975, pp. 111-119.

**226**

Van der Spak, P. G.

"Mexico's Booming Border Zone: a Magnet for Labor-Intensive
American Plants." *Inter-American Economic Affairs* (29: 2),
1975, pp. 33-47.

**227**

Bustamante, Jorge A.

*Maquiladoras: A New Face of International Capitalism on Mexi-
co's Northern Frontier*. Paper, Sixth National Meetings of the
Latin American Studies Association, Atlanta, GA, March 23-24,
1975.

**228**

Gollás, M.

"Reflexiones Sobre la Concentración Económica y el Crecimiento de las Empresas." México, *Trimestre Económico* (42:
166), April-June 1975, p. 457-485.

**229**

Teutli Otero, G.

"Les Industries 'Maquiladoras': Progrès ou Régression dans le
Processus Méxicain de Développement." Paris, *Tiers Monde* 16,
April-June 1975, pp. 381-406.

**230**

Barkin, David

"Mexico's Albatross: the United States Economy." Riverside,
CA, *Latin American Perspectives* 2, Summer 1975, pp. 64-80.

**231**

"México: Empresas Maquiladoras de Exportación, por Ciudades."
México, *El Mercado de Valores* (35: 25) June 23, 1975, p. 521.
("Por Ciudades," in first table; "Por Productos Procesados,"
second table on same page; both correspond to the year 1974.)

**232**

"Border Plants Hit by Labor Costs." *Industrial Development* 144,
July 1975, pp. 27-28.

**233**

Butler, M. T.
  "Border Industries: Inflation in Mexico and Recession in U.S.
  Threatens Maquiladora Accomplishments." *Federal Reserve
  Dallas Business Review*, July 1975, pp. 1-7.

**234**

Inman, H,. A., & Ortiz Tirado, A.
  "Mexican Dividend: 'las Maquiladoras.'" *The International
  Lawyer* 9, July 1975, pp. 431-440.

**235**

"Hit and run: U.S. Runaway Shops on the Mexican Border." New
York, *Latin American & Empire Report* (NACLA), 9, July-August 1975, pp. 1-30.

**236**

Bjur, W. E.
  "International Manager and the Third Sector." *Public Administration Review* 35, September 1975, pp. 463-467.

**237**

Brill, D. H., Jr.
  "Mexican Law and Policy on Foreign Investment and Transfer-
  ence of Technology." Paris, *Droit et Pratique du Commerce International* (1: 3), September 1975, pp. 383-394.

**238**

Meyers, H. B.

"That Incredible Economy South of the Border." *Fortune* 92, September 1975, pp. 112-116.

**239**

Baerressen, D. W.

"Unemployment and Mexico's Border Industrialization Program." *Inter-American Economic Affairs* 29, Autumn 1975, pp. 79-90.

**240**

Evans, John S.

"The Use of Incentives for the Development of Mexico's Northern Border Zone." *El Paso Economic Review* 12, October 1975, pp. 1-4.

**241**

Bustamante, Jorge A.

"El Programa Fronterizo de Maquiladoras: Observaciones para una Evaluación." México, *Foro Internacional* (16: 2), October-December 1975, pp. 183-204.

**242**

Fainzylber, F.

"Las Empresas Transnacionales y el Sistema Industrial de México." México, *Trimestre Económico* (42: 4), October-December 1975, pp. 903-931.

**243**

Tienda, Marta

"Diferencias Socioeconomicas Regionales y Tasas de Participación de la Fuerza de Trabajo Femenina: el Caso de México." México, *Revista Mexicana de Sociología* (37: 4), October-December 1975, pp. 911-929.

**244**

Urquidi, V., & Mendez Villareal, Sofía

"Importancia Económica de la Zona Fronteriza del Norte de

México." México, *Foro Internacional* (16: 2), October-December 1975, pp. 149-176.

**245**

Rohan, T. M.
"Customs Woes Hurting Mexican Border Plants." *Industry Week* 187, November 10, 1975, pp. 14-16.

**246**

Slocum, K. G.
"A Problem of Pesos: U.S. Concerns Worry That Soaring Wages in Mexico may Hurt Border-Plant Profit." *Wall Street Journal* 186, November 21, 1975, p. 48.

**247**

"Mexico: Expanding Trade, Investment Opportunities." *Journal of Commerce* 326, November 24, 1975, 1-A, 15-A.

*1976*

**248**

Bustamante, Jorge A.
"Maquiladoras: a New Face of International Capitalism in Mexico's Northern Frontier." Paper presented at the Latin American Studies Association Conference, Atlanta, GA, March 1976.

**249**

Cehelsky, Marta
"The U.S.-Mexico Border Areas as a Development Region." Paper presented to the Southwestern Social Science Association Meeting, Dallas, TX, April 1976.

**250**

Dillman, C. D.
"Mexico's Border Industrialization Program (BIP): Current Patterns and Alternative Futures." Paper presented at Latin American Studies Association Conference, Atlanta, GA, March 1976.

**251**

Dillman, C. D.
"Mexico's In-Bond Assembly Plants: Impact, Problems and Prospects." Paper presented at Conference of Latin Americanist Geographers, University of Texas at El Paso, October, 1976.

**252**

Fainzylber, F., & Martínez Tarragó, Trinidad
*Las Empresas Transnacionales: Expansión a Nivel Mundial y Proyección en la Industria Mexicana*. México, Fondo de Cultura Económica, 1976, 423p.

**253**

Gollás, M., & García, Adalberto
"El Desarrollo Económico Reciento de México" (In: Wilkie, James W. et al., eds. *Contemporary Mexico: Papers of the Fourth International Congress of Mexican History*. Berkeley: University of California Press, 1976, pp. 405-440).

**254**

Grigoreva, Z. K.
*Innostrannyj Kapital v Ekonomike Meksiki. (Foreign Capital in the Mexican Economy)*. Moscow, Nauka, 1976, 159p.

**255**

México. Dirección General de Promoción y Asuntos Internacionales. Depto de Asuntos Fronterizos *Información Relativa Sobre las Empresas Maquiladoras, Establecidas en el País*. México, 1976.

**256**

México. Secretaría de Industria y Comercio
*Monografías Socioeconómicas de las Ciudades Fronterizas*. México, 1976, 122p.

**257**

México. Secretaría de Industria y Comercio
*Programa Fronterizo: Seis Años de Acción Coordinada*. México, 1976, 57p.

**258**

*Monografías Socioeconómicas de las Ciudades Fronterizas, México, 1976.* México, Talleres Gráficas de la Nación, 1976, 122p.

**259**

Rosado, Margarita R.
*La Condición de las Obreras en las Maquiladoras de la Frontera Norte.* Tesis Profesional. México, El Colegio de México, 1976.

**260**

Sepúlveda, César
*La Frontera Norte de México* . . . México, Ed. Porrúa, 1976, 171p.

**260-A**

Unikel, Luis et al.
*El Desarrollo Urbano de México: Diagnóstico e Implicaciones Futuras.* México: Centro de Estudios Económicos y Demográficos, El Colegio de México, 1976, 466p.

**261**

*A View of the Border From Mexico; Proceedings of a Conference, San Diego, CA, May 7-8, 1976/Fronteras 1976.* San Diego, Fronteras, 1976, 36p.

**262**

Dillman, C. D.
"Maquiladoras in Mexico's Northern Border Communities and the Border Industrialization Program." Rotterdam, *Tijdschrift voor Economische en Sociale Geographie* (67: 3), 1976, pp. 138-150.

**263**

Paredes Lopez, O., & Gallardo Navarro, Y.
"La Industria Alimentaria en México y la Penetración de las Empresas Transnacionales." México, *Comercio Exterior* (26: 12), 1976, pp. 1421-1435.

**264**
Weinert, R. S.
"Multinationals in Latin America." *Journal of Inter-American Studies* 18, 1976, pp. 253-260.

**265**
"Comercio Exterior." Madrid, *Información Comercial Española*, January 1976, pp. 76-123.

**266**
Trejo Reyes, S.
"Expansión Industrial y Empleo en México, 1965-1970." México, *Trimestre Económico* (43: 1), January-March 1976, pp. 37-56.

**267**
Zazueta, C.
"Empresas Transnacionales: una Tésis para el Estado." México, *Pensamiento Político* 21, February 1976, pp. 225-234.

**268**
"Report Says Mexico Attractive to Foreign Investors." *Los Angeles Times*, February 2, 1976, section 3, p. 10, column 6.

**269**
"Laredo, Texas Paso Libre American Promotion Viewed." *Los Angeles Times*, February 22, 1976, section 1, p. 1, column 3.

**270**
Amador Leal, A.
"Desarrollo Tecnológico: Antecedentes y Perspectivas." México, *Pensamiento Político* (21: 84), April 1976, pp. 491-498.

**270-A**
Palerm, Angel
"Los Beneficiarios del Desarrollo Regional." México: *Pensamiento Político* 21, April 1976, pp. 535-550.

**271**

McCaughan, Ed.
"U.S. Shops Running Away." Bellingham, WA, *Northwest Passage* (14: 1), April 26, 1976, p. 9.

**272**

"Re Runaway Shops." San Francisco, *Common Sense* (3: 7), May 1976, p. 15.

**273**

Hoover, J.
"Corporations and Mexican Industry." Paris, *Direct From Cuba* 50, August 1, 1976, p. 39.

**274**

"U.S. Business/Mexican Harvest." Portland, OR, *Portland Scribe* (5: 22), September 2, 1976, p. 5.

**275**

"Mexico Seeks to Expand Exports to U.S." *Los Angeles Times*, September 8, 1976, section 3, p. 13, column 1.

**276**

Duncan, C.
"The Runaway Shop and the Mexican Border Industrialization Program." *Southwest Economy and Society* 2, October-November 1976, pp. 4-25.

**276-A**

Carrillo Flores, Antonio
"Testimonio Sobre el Debate Constitucional que Suscitó la Convención del Chamizal de 1963." México: *Memoria de El Colegio Nacional* (8: 2), December 1976, pp. 1406-1413. (speech delivered by the Hon. Antonio Carrillo Flores, Mexican Ministry of Foreign Affairs)

**276-B**

Pedrão, Fernando
"La Experiencia del Proyecto de Desarrollo Regional y Urbano

de México." México: *Comercio Exterior* (26: 12), 1976, pp. 1398-1405.

**276-C**
Ramírez Rancaño, Mario
"Evolución del Empresario Imperialista en la Economía Mexicana." Barranquilla, Colombia: *Desarrollo Indoamericano* 12, December 1976, pp. 49-53.

**277**
Torres, Olga E.
"Algunas Observaciones Sobre la Economía de la Frontera Norte de México." México, *Comercio Exterior* (26: 12), December 1976, pp. 1406-1413.

**278**
"Mexico and U.S. Sign $99 Million Trade Agreement." *Los Angeles Times*, December 3, 1976, section 1, p. 22, column 1.

**279**
"Mexico/U.S. Multinationals Provoke Storm." Berkeley, CA, *People's World* (39: 49), December 4, 1976, p. 1.

**280**
"Uncertainty About Political and Economic Situation Hurts Tijuana." *Los Angeles Times*, December 10, 1976, section 1, p. 3, column 5.

*1977*

**281**
Aguilar Monteverde, A. et al.
*Politica Mexicana Sobre Inversiones Extranjeras*. México, Instituto de Investigaciones Económicas, Universidad Nacional Autónoma de México, 1977, 249p.

**282**
Boatler, Robert W.
*The Technology-Adoption-Adjustment Model of Mexico's Manufactured Exports: Theoretical and Empirical Extensions* (Work-

ing Paper #77-33). Austin, Graduate School of Business, University of Texas, 1977, 11p.

**283**
Campero V., Marta P., & Guerrero, Carmen A.
"Reflexiones sobre la participación de la obrera de la industria maquiladora en Mexicali, Baja California, y su impacto en la estructura familiar." Paper presented at Simposio Centroamericano sobre la Mujer, México, D.F., noviembre, 1977.

**284**
Escamilla, Norma, & Vigorito, Maria A.
*Consideraciones Sociológicas del Trabajo Femenino en las Maquiladoras Fronterizas*. Research Report. Mexicali, Universidad Autónoma de Baja California, Escuela de Ciencias Sociales y Políticas, 1977.

**285**
Fernandez, R. A.
*The United States-Mexico Border: A Politico-Economic Profile*. Notre Dame, IN, University of Notre Dame Press, 1977, 174p.

**286**
India. Indian Institute of Foreign Trade
*Export Promotion Measures in Mexico, Brazil and South Korea*. New Delhi, 1977, 203p.

**287**
Matthies, Klaus
*Transnationale Unternehmen in Mexiko*. Hamburg, Federal Republic of Germany, Verlag Weltarchiv, 1977, 185p.

**287-A**
Nadal Egea, Alejandro
*Instrumentos de Política Científica y Tecnología en México*. México: Centro de Estudios Económicos y Demográficos, El Colegio de México, 1977, 309p.

**287-B**
*Política Mexicana Sobre Inversiones*. México: Instituto de Investigaciones Económicas, Seminario de Teoría del Desarrollo, Un-

iversidad Nacional Autónoma de México (cuaderno #4), 1977, 249p.

**288**

Siebert, D. D., & Zaidi, M. A.
*The Role of the new Industrial Towns in the Development of Mexico*. Minneapolis, Industrial Relations Center, University of Minnesota, 1977, 42p. (Working Paper #77-09).

**289**

Texas. Legislature. Senate. Special Committee on Border Trade & Tourism
*Report to the 65th Legislature of the Senate Special Committee on Border Trade and Tourism*. Austin, The Committee, 1977, 9 & 20pp.

**290**

U.S. Senate. Committee on Foreign Relations. Subcommittee on Foreign Economic Policy
*Market Power and Profitability of Multinational Corporations in Brazil and Mexico:* Report April 1977, by John M. Connor & Willard F. Mueller. 95th Congress, 1st Session. Committee Print. Washington, 1977, 136p.

**291**

Caputo, O.
"La Inversión Extranjera Directa, las Empresas Multinacionales, y el Empleo Directo en México." México, *Investigación Económica*, nueva época (36: 1), 1977, pp. 157-204.

**292**

Martínez, Oscar J.
"Chicanos and the Border Cities: an Interpretive Essay." *Pacific Historical Review* (46: 1), 1977, pp. 85-106.

**292-A**

Boltvinik, Julio
"La Política de Ciencia y Tecnología en México." México: *Investigatión Económica*, new series (36: 2), 1977, pp. 183-198.

**293**

Greenwood, M. J., & Ladman, J.
"Economía de la Mobilidad Geográfica de la Mano de Obra en México." México, *Demografía y Economía* (11: 2), 1977, pp. 155-166.

**294**

Sloan, John W., & West, Jonathan P.
"The Role of Informal Policy Making in U.S.-Mexico Border Cities." *Social Science Quarterly* (58: 2), September 1977, pp. 270-282.

**295**

Ingles, G., & Fairchild, Loretta
"Evaluating the Impact of Foreign Investment: Methodology and the Evidence From Mexico, Colombia and Brazil." *Latin American Research Review* (12: 3), 1977, pp. 57-70.

**296**

Nuñoz, María E., & Murayama, Guadalupe
"Las Obreras y la Industria Maquiladora." México, *FEM* (Nueva Cultura Feminista, A.C.) (1: 3), 1977, pp. 40-46.

**296-A**

Herrera, Ligia
"Tasa de Crecimiento y Deterioro del Medio Urbano en México: un Intento Exploratorio de las Relaciones Existentes." México: *Demografía y Economía* (11: 3), 1977, pp. 259-272.

**297**

Tienda, Marta
"Diferenciación Regional y Transformación Sectorial de la Mano de Obra Femenina en México, 1970." México, *Demografía y Economía* (11: 3), 1977, pp. 307-325.

**298**

Bustamante, Jorge A.
"El Debate Sobre la 'Invasión Silenciosa'." México, *Foro Internacional* (17: 3), January-March 1977, pp. 403-417.

**299**
Dillman, C. D.
"Commuter Workers in the Borderlands—1967." *Frontera* 2, March, 1977, pp. 7-8.

**300**
Seremetev, I. K.
"Tendencii Razvitija Nacional'noj Ekonomiki" ("Development Trends in the National Economy"). Moscow, *Latinskaja America* (8: 2), March-April 1977, pp. 27-45.

**301**
James, M.
"Jobs on the Line in Texas Border Tug of War." *Worklife* 2, May 1977, pp. 2-5.

**302**
Unger, K.
"Algunas Observaciones Sobre Transferencia de Tecnología en dos Sectores de Manufacturas." México, *Trimestre Económico* (44: 2), April-June 1977, pp. 483-500.

**303**
Alba, F.
"Condiciones y Políticas Económicas en la Frontera Norte de México." *Natural Resources Journal* 17, October 1977, pp. 571-584.

**304**
Dixon, J.
"Mexican Connection." *Distribution Worldwide* 76, October 1977, pp. 79-82.

**305**
Fairchild, Loretta
"Performance and Technology of U.S. National Firms in Mexico." *Journal of Development Studies* (14: 1), October 1977, pp. 14-34.

**306**
"Fomento de la Industria Maquiladora" (*Reglamento del Párrafo Tercero del Artículo 32 del Código Aduanero de los Estados Unidos Mexicanos para el Fomento de la Industria Maquiladora*). México, *El Mercado de Valores* (37: 46), November 14, 1977, pp. 887-892.

**207**
Jenkins, R.
"Foreign Firms, Manufactured Exports and Development Strategy: the Case of Mexico." Amsterdam, Holland, *Boletín de Estudios Latinoamericanos y del Caríbe* (CEDLA), December 1977, pp. 69-95.

**308**
Rohan, T. M.
"Business Booming for Mexican Border Plants." *Industry Week* 195, December 5, 1977, p. 26.

*1978*

**309**
Gildersleeve, C. R.
*The International Border City: Urban Spatial Organization in a Context of Two Cultures Along the United States-Mexico Boundary*. Lincoln, NE, 1978, 374p. (Ph.D. Dissertation, University of Nebraska).

**309-A**
International Labour Organisation. Programa Regional de Empleo para América Latina y el Caríbe (PREALC)
*Opciones de Políticas y Creación de Empleo Productivo en México*. Santiago, Chile: 1978, 84p.

**310**
Martínez, Oscar J.
*Foreign Domination of Mexico's Northern Border Region: A Historical Look at Ciudad Juarez*. Paper, Primer Simposio Internacional Sobre Los Problemas de Los Trabajadores Indocu-

mentados de Mexico y Los Estados Unidos, Guadalajara, Jalisco, Mexico, 1978.

**311**
Martínez, Oscar J.
*Border Boom Town: Ciudad Juarez Since 1848*. Austin, TX, University of Texas Press, 1978, 231p.

**312**
Mitchell, Jacquelyn A.
*Preliminary Report on the Impact of Mexico's Twin Plant Industry Along the United States-Mexico Border*. El Paso, TX, Organization of U.S. Border Cities, 1978.

**313**
Nafari, Akbar
*United States Multinational Corporations in Mexican Manufacturing: a Study of Development and Balance of Payments Impacts*. Bloomington, IN, 1978, 232p. (Ph.D. Dissertation, Indiana University)

**314**
Nolasco, Margarita A.
*Frontera Norte*. Paper Presented at the Primer Simposio Internacional Sobre los Problemas de los Trabajadores Indocumentados de México y los Estados Unidos, Guadalajara, México, 1978.

**315**
Ramírez Torres, Olga E.
*La Economía de Frontera: el Caso de la Frontera Norte de México*. Mexico, Impresiones Aries, 1978, 120p.

**316**
Ross, James K.
*El Paso, Texas Foreign Trade Zone Economic Feasibility Study*. El Paso: Allan L. Lemley & Associates, 1978.

**317**
Trajtenberg, Raúl
*Transnacionales y Fuerza de Trabajo en la Periferia; Tenden-*

*cias Recientes en la Internacionalización de la Producción.*
México: Instituto Latinoamericano de Estudios Transnacionales,
1978, 59p.

## 317-A
Angeles, Luis
"Notas Sobre el Comportamiento Reciente de la Inversión
Privada en México." México; *Comercio Exterior* (28:1), 1978,
pp. 11-23.

## 318
Boseman, F. G., & Phatak, A.
"Management Practices of Industrial Enterprises in Mexico: a
Comparative Study." Wiesbaden, Germany, *Management International Review* (18: 1), 1978, pp. 43-49.

## 318-A
Clavijo, Fernando et al.
"A qué Modelo de Industrialización Corresponden las Exportaciones Mexicanas?" México: *Trimestre Económico* (45: 1),
1978, pp. 109-135.

## 319
Gordon, M. W.
"The Joint Venture as an Institution for Mexican Development: a
Legislative History." *Arizona State Law Journal 1978*, nos. 2/3,
1978, pp. 173-203.

## 320
Howe, Carolyn
"Multinationals and Labor Unity: Both Sides." *Southwest Economics & Sociology* (4: 1), 1978, pp. 43-74.

## 321
Mentz, A.
"Problème des Mexikanischen Gesetzes uber Auslandische Investitionen." Heidelberg, Germany, *Recht der Internationaler
Wirtschaft* (24: 3), 1978, pp. 155-160.

**322**
Revel-Mouroz, J.
Économie Frontalière et Organisation de l'Espace: Réflexions à Partir de l'Exemple de la Frontière Méxique-États Unis.'' Paris, *Cahiers des Amériques Latines* 18, 1978, pp. 7-16.

**323**
Cabrera, C.
"El Desarrollo Económico de Tijuana en Relación al Suministro de Agua y a la Contaminación Atmosférica, Marina y Acuática." *Natural Resources Journal* 18, January 1978, pp. 11-27.

**324**
Dillman, C. D.
"Assembly Plants and Multinational Corporations in Mexico." Paper presented to the Association of American Geographers Meeting, New Orleans, LA, April 1978.

**325**
Hoffman, P. R.
"The Internal Structure of Mexican Border Cities." Paper presented the Association of American Geographers, New Orleans, LA, April 1978.

**326**
"La Industria Maquiladora: Evolución Reciente y Perspectivas." México, *Comercio Exterior* (28: 4), April 1978, pp. 407-414.

**327**
Juarez, Antonio, & Villarespe, Verónica
*La Instalación de Plantas Maquiladoras en México; un Caso de Anexión Económica*. Paper, Primer Simposio Internacional Sobre los Problemas de los Trabajadores Indocumentados de México y los Estados Unidos, Guadalajara, México, April 1978.

**328**
Margulis, Mario
"Petroleo, Indocumentados y Maquiladoras: Teoría de la Renta y Transferencia de Valor." México, *Arte, Sociedad Ideología* 6, April-May 1978, pp. 103-119.

**329**
Gollás, M.
"Estructura y Causas de la Concentración Industrial en México." México, *Trimestre Económico* (45: 2), April-June 1978, pp. 325-356.

**330**
Gordon, D.
"Mexico, a Survey." *The Economist* 267, April 22, 1978, pp. 1-34.

**331**
Fernandez Kelly, Maria P.
"Mexican Border Industrialization: Female Labor Force Participation and Migration." Paper presented at Meeting of the American Sociological Association, San Francisco, CA, September 1978.

**331-A**
Ferreira, Héctor
"Una Aproximación al Análisis Regional del Desarrollo Industrial." México: *Comercio Exterior* (28: 10), 1978, pp. 1225-1233.

**331-B**
Platon, Pierre
"Le Méxique Peut Offrir aux Investisseurs Français d'Intéressantes Perspectives." Paris, *Industries et Travaux d'Outremer* 26, October 1978, pp. 764-767.

**332**
Chernow, R.
"When Jobs Go South." San Francisco, *Mother Jones* (3: 9), November 1978, p. 53.

**333**
"Mexico: the Opportunity Is Now." *Business Week*, November 6, 1978, pp. 37-54.

**334**
"U.S.-Mexican Border Industrialization Program Viewed." *Los Angeles Times*, November 6, 1978, section 3, p. 15, column 4.

**335**
Prieto, J.
"The Challenge of the U.S.-Mexico Border." *Christian Century* 95, December 27, 1978, pp. 1258-1262.

## *1979*

**336**
Baird, Peter, & McCaughan, Ed
*Beyond the Border: Mexico and the United States Today; with Investment Profile by Marc Herold* . . . New York, NACLA, 1979, 205p.

**337**
Barrera Bassols, J.
"Frontera Norte: Maquiladoras y Migración" (In: *Aspectos Sociales de la Migración en México*, v. 2. México, Instituto Nacional de Antropología e Historia, 1979, pp. 295-315).

**338**
Bassols Batalla, A.
*México: Formación de Regiones Económicas: Influencias, Factores y Sistemas*. México, Universidad Nacional Autónoma de México, 1979, 625p.

**339**
Business International Corp., New York
*The Effects of Foreign Investment on Selected Host Countries: a Special Research Study*. New York, 1979, 196p.

**340**
Campero V., Marta P., & Guerrero, Carmen A.
*Fuerza de trabajo en la industria maquiladora: Modificaciones en el paper familiar de la mujer obrera*. Tesis profesional. Escuela de Ciencias Sociales y Políticas, Universidad Autónoma de Baja California, Mexicali, Baja California, 1979.

**341**
Coyle, Laurie et al.
*Women at FARAH: an Unfinished Story*. El Paso, TX, El Paso
Chapter of Bibliotecarios al Servicio del Pueblo, 1979, 66p.

**342**
De la Rosa Hickerson, Gustavo
"La Contratacion Colectiva en las Maquiladoras: Análisis de un
caso de Sobreexplotación." Tesis profesional. Universidad
Autónoma de Ciudad Juárez, Ciudad Juárez, Chihauhua, 1979.

**343**
Fernandez Kelly, Maria P.
"Women in Mexican Border Industries: the Search for Cheap
Labor." Paper presented at the 78th Annual Meeting of the
American Anthropological Association, Cincinnati, 1979.

**344**
Gambrill, Monica C.
"Composición y Consciencia de la Fuerza de Trabajo en la Ma-
quiladora." Paper presented at Simposio Nacional Sobre Estu-
dios Fronterizos, Universidad Autónoma de Nuevo León y El
Colegio de México, Monterrey, N.L., 24-27 de enero, 1979.

**345**
Goodman, Paul W., & Rivera, Julius
"Institutionalization of Border Legal and Illegal Relationships"
(Paper delivered at the Southwestern Sociological Association
Conference, 1979).

**346**
Hansen, Niles
*The Role of Mexican Labor in the Economy of the Southwest
United States*. Austin, Mexico-United States Border Research
Program, Southwest Borderlands Regional Economic Develop-
ment Program, 1979, 52p.

**347**
König, W.
*Efectos de la Actividad Maquiladora Fronteriza en la Sociedad*

*Mexicana*. Paper Presented at the Simposio Nacional Sobre Estudios de El Colegio de México y Facultad de Filosofía y Letras de la Universidad Autónoma de Nuevo León, Monterrey, N.L., México, January 24-27, 1979.

**348**
Marquez, V. B. de, comp.
*Dinámica de la Empresa Mexicana: Perspectivas Políticas, Económicas y Sociales*. Mexico, El Colegio de México, 1979, 442p.

**349**
Mendoza Berrueto, E.
*Historia de los Programas Federales para el Desarrollo Económico de la Frontera Norte*. Ciudad Juarez, Mexico [s.n.] 1979, 63p.

**350**
México. Secretaría del Patrimonio Industrial y Fomentación
*Indicadores Socioeconómicos de la Industria Maquiladora en México*. México, 1979.

**350-A**
Montavon, Rémy et al.
*L'Implantation de Deux Entreprises Multinationales au México*. Paris: Presses Universitaires de France, 1979, 168p.

**351**
Müller, Ronald E.
"The Multinational Corporation and the Underdevelopment of the Third World" (In: Wilbur, Charles K., ed. *The Political Economy of Development and Underdevelopment*. New York, Random House, 1979, pp. 151-178).

**352**
México. Secretaría de Hacienda y Crédito Público
*Aspectos Dinámicos de la Economía Mexicana: un Modelo Macroeconómico*. México, Dirección General de Planeación Hacendaria, 1979.

**353**
United Nations. Industrial Development Organization
*Industrial Priorities in Developing Countries: the Selection Process in Brazil, India, Mexico, Republic of Korea, and Turkey.*
New York, United Nations, 1979, 180p.

**354**
Ladman, J.
"The Economic Interdependence of Contiguous Border Cities: the Twin City Multiplier." *Annals of Regional Science* 13, 1979, pp. 23-28.

**355**
Revel-Mouroz, Jean
"Mobilité du Travail ou Mobilité du Capital? Accords et Conflits à la Frontière Méxique-États Unis." Paris: *Problèmes d'Amérique Latine* 53, 1979, pp. 45-75.

**356**
Revel-Mouroz, J., & Vanneph, Alian
"Enclave Petrolière et Enclave Frontalière dans le Nord-Est du Méxique: Reynosa." Paris, *Cahiers des Amériques Latines* 20, 1979, pp. 95-110.

**357**
Bustamante, Jorge A.
"El Estudio de la Zona Fronteriza México-Estados Unidos." México, *Foro Internacional* 19, January-March 1979, pp. 471-516.

**358**
Srodes, J.
"Mexico: is it as Good as it Looks?" *Financial World* 148, March 15, 1979, pp. 53-56.

**359**
Garnier, G. et al.
"Autonomy of the Mexican Affiliates of U.S. Multinational Corporations: Decision Making in Foreign Affiliates: Centralized

or Decentralized?'' *Columbia Journal of World Business* 14, Spring 1979, pp. 78-90.

**360**
''Carey McWilliams Article on Proposed North American Common Market.'' *Los Angeles Times*, April 8, 1979, section 6, p. 3, column 1-C.

**361**
''New Interest in Mexican Plants.'' *Industry Week* 201, April 16, 1979, pp. 42-43.

**362**
Jenkins, R.
''Export Performance of Multinational Corporations in Mexican Industry.'' London, *Journal of Development Studies* 15, April 1979, pp. 89-107.

**363**
Charlot, F. S.
''Le Contrôle des Investissements Étrangers et des Transferts de Technologie au Méxique.'' Paris, *Droit et Pratique du Commerce International*, June 1979, pp. 309-320.

**364**
Schooler, R. D., & Gonzalez Arce, J.
''Attitudes of Border Residents Toward United States-Mexico Border Industrialization.'' *Missouri State University Business Topics* (17: 3), Summer 1979.

**365**
McClelland, E. L.
''U.S.-Mexico Border Industry Back on Fast-Growth Track.'' *Federal Reserve Bank of Dallas Voice*, July 1979, pp. 3-9.

**366**
Gambrill, Monica C.
''Maquiladoras: el Costas de Sus Trabajadores.'' México, *Boletín Informativo Sobre Asuntos Migratorios y Fronterizos* 7, July-August 1979, pp. 6-8.

**367**

"Huelga de Trabajadores en una Maquiladora en Tijuana." México, *Boletín Informativo del Comité de Servicio de los Amigos* #7, July-August 1979, p. 10.

**368**

"Feature on Growth of U.S. Manufacturing 'Thin Plants' Inside Mexican Line." *Los Angeles Times*, September 19, 1979, section 1, p. 1, column 1.

**369**

Van Slambrouch, Paul
"Business Jumps Mexican Border." *Christian Science Monitor*, September 21, 1979, p. 2, column 1.

**370**

"Canada and Mexico Unenthusiastic Over Common North American Market Plan." *Los Angeles Times*, September 30, 1979, section 4, p. 1, column 3.

**371**

Flanigan, J.
"Mexico's Drive to Industrialize." *Forbes* 124, October 29, 1979, pp. 41-49.

**372**

Revel-Mouroz, J.
"Mobilité de Travail ou Mobilité du Capital? Accords et Conflits à la Frontière." Aubervilliers Cedex, France, *Notes et Études Documentaires* (Série: Problèmes d'Amérique Latine), 4533/4534, October 31, 1979, pp. 45-75.

**373**

"Mujeres y Transnacionales en Ciudad Juarez." México, *Boletín Informativo Sobre Asuntos Migratorios y Fronterizos* 9, November-January 1979/80, pp. 12-13.

**374**

"Mexico: Frontier of the '80's." *Business Week*, November 5, 1979, pp. 23-46.

**375**
"Small Mexican Village Chosen as Focal Point of Industrial Revolution." *Los Angeles Times*, November 25, 1979, section 4, p. 6, column 1.

**376**
Seay, Janice, & Trejo, Larry
"Is the Border Twin-Plant Concept for you?" *Texas Business* (4: 6), December 1979, pp. 55-56.

**377**
Spaeth, A.
"Maquila Boom; U.S.-Owned Factories." *Forbes* 124, December 10, 1979, pp. 102-104.

## *1980*

**378**
Arriola Woog, Mario, & Tiano, Susan B.
*El Programa Mexicano de Maquiladoras: una Respuesta a las Necesidades de la Industria Norteamericana*. Guadalajara, México: Universidad de Guadalajara, Instituto de Estudios Sociales, 1980, 134p.

**379**
Carrillo Viveros, Jorge
*La Utilizacion de la Mano de Obra Femenina en la Industria Maquiladora: el Case de Ciudad Juarez*. Preliminary Research Report. México, Colegio de México, Programa de Estudios de la Frontera y los Estados Unidos, 1980.

**380**
Fernandez Kelly, Maria P.
*"Chavalas de Maquiladora": a Study of the Female Labor Force in Ciudad Juarez's Offshore Production Plants*. New Brunswick, NJ, 1980, 402p. (Ph.D. Dissertation, Rutgers University)

**381**
Flamm, Kenneth S.
*Technology, Employment and Direct Foreign Investment: Evidence From the Mexican Manufacturing Sector.* Cambridge, MA: 1980, 182p. (Ph.D. Dissertation, Massachusetts Institute of Technology)

**382**
Froebel, Folker et al.
*The new International Division of Labor: Structural Unemployment in Industrialized Countries and Industrialization in Developing Countries.* Translated by Peter Burgess. New York, Cambridge University Press, 1980, 407p.

**383**
Garza, Gustavo
*Industrialización de las Principales Ciudades de México; Hacia una Estrategia Espacio-Sectorial de Descentralización Industrial.* México, El Colegio de México, 1980, 155p.

**384**
Hernandez, Alberto
*Política y Práctica Laboral en la Industria Maquiladora: el Caso de Ciudad Juarez.* Research Report. México, El Colegio de México, Programa de Estduios de la Frontera y los Estados Unidos, 1980.

**385**
"Internalization of Capital and Labor in Mexico's In-Bond 'Maquiladora' Industry." Paper presented at Simposio Interdisciplinario sobre la Inversión Extranjera en México, Universidad Nacional Autónoma de México, México, 20 de febrero, 1980.

**386**
*International Issues: Mexico and the United States, April 9-11, 1980.* Conference sponsored by the Stanley Foundation, Muscatine, IA. Muscatine, IA, Stanley Foundation, 1980, 18p.

**387**
Jamail, Milton H.
*United States-Mexican Border: A Guide to Institutions, Organizations and Scholars*. Tucson, Latin American Area Center, University of Arizona, 1980, 153p.

**388**
Peña, Devon G.
*Female Workers and Trade Unionism in the Mexican Border Industrialization Program*. Paper, Eighth Annual Meeting of the National Association for Chicano Studies, Houston, TX, April 17-19, 1980.

**389**
Story, Dale
*Entrepreneurs and the State in Mexico: Examining the Authoritarian Thesis*. Austin, Office for Public Sector Studies, Institute of Latin American Studies, University of Texas, 1980, 14p.

**390**
Hernandez, Laos, E.
"Economías Extranjeras y el Proceso de Concentración Regional de la Industria en México." México, *Trimestre Económico* (47: 1), 1980, pp. 119-157.

**391**
"Multinational Mexican Workers: Their Struggles, the Multidimensional Attack on Them, and Possible Responses." *Zerowork: Political Materials* 3, 1980.

**392**
"Ni a Sueldo Mínimo Llegamos: Hablan Obreras de la Máquina Textil." México, *Boletín Informativo Sobre Asuntos Migratorios y Fronterizos* 12, 1980, pp. 6-7.

**393**
Sanchez Cordero, D. J. A.
"La Industrialización." México, *Anuario Jurídico* 7, 1980, pp. 217-225.

**394**

Wilson, L. C.

"Settlement of Boundary Disputes: Mexico, the United States and the International Boundary Commission." London: *International & Comparative Law Quarterly* 29, January 1980, pp. 38-53.

**395**

"Plan Global de Desarrollo." México, *Problemas del Desarrollo* (11: 41), January-April 1980, pp. 9-30.

**396**

Rigg, Howard V.

"The Maquila Program." *Revista Inteamericana de Bibliografía* (10: 1), Spring 1980, pp. 83-93.

**397**

Mercado García, A. et al.

"Un Estudio Sobre la Transferencia de Tecnología en la Industria Mexicana del Vestido." México, *Demografía y Economía* (14: 2), April-June 1980, pp. 179-213.

**398**

"Multinationals Press on Quietly in Mexico." *Advertising Age* 51, section 2, May 12, 1980, p. S-24.

**399**

"Future Boom Along Road Paralle to New Mexico-Mexico Border Viewed." *Los Angeles Times*, May 18, 1980, section 9, p. 4, column 1.

**400**

Kryzda, B. F.

"Joint Ventures and Technology Transfers." *Case Western Reserve Journal of International Law*, Summer 1980, pp. 549-573.

**401**

Plattner, S.

"Economic Development and Occupational Change in a Developing Area of Mexico." *Journal of Developing Areas* 14, July 1980, pp. 1469-1481.

**402**

Seib, Gerald

"Pipeline, Power Plants, Factories Transform Mexico's U.S. Border." *Wall Street Journal*, July 15, 1980, section 2, pp. 33-W, 29-E. column 1.

**403**

Gambrill, Monica C.

"El Trabajo de las Mujeres en la Industria de la Máquila." México, *Boletín Informativo Sobre Asuntos Migratorios y Fronterizos* 13, August-September 1980, pp. 5-7.

**401**

Plattner, S.

"Economic Development and Occupational Change in a Developing Area of Mexico." *Journal of Developing Areas* 14, July 1980, pp. 1469-1481.

**402**

Seib, Gerald

"Pipeline, Power Plants, Factories Transform Mexico's U.S. Border." *Wall Street Journal*, July 15, 1980, section 2, pp. 33-W, 29-E. column 1.

**403**

Gambrill, Monica C.

"El Trabajo de las Mujeres en la Industria de la Máquila." México, *Boletín Informativo Sobre Asuntos Migratorios y Fronterizos* 13, August-September 1980, pp. 5-7.

**404**

Gonzalez Casanova, P.

"The Economic Development of Mexico." *Scientific American* 243, September 1980, pp. 192-196.

**405**

Peña, Devon G.

"Las Maquiladoras: Mexican Women and Class Struggle in the Border Industries." *Aztlan* (11: 2), Fall 1980, pp. 159-229.

**406**
Weintraub, Sidney
"North American Free Trade." *Challenge* 23, September-October 1980, pp. 48-51.

**407**
Peña, Devon G.
"Las Maquiladores: Mexican Women and Class Struggles in the Border Industries." *Aztlan* (11: 2), Fall 1980, pp. 159-229.

**408**
Kelly, P.
"The Maquila Women." New York, *NACLA's Report on the Americas* (14: 5), October 1980, p. 14.

**409**
"La Lucha de las Obreras de la Maquiladora Convertors S.A. de C.V. en Ciudad Juarez." México, *Boletín Informativo Sobre Asuntos Migratorios y Fronterizos* 14, October-December 1980, pp. 9-10.

**410**
Olmedo Carranza, Bernardo
"Inversiones Extranjeras y Empresas Transnacionales." México, *Problemas del Desarrollo* (40: 10), November 1979-January 1980, pp. 107-115.

*1981*

**411**
Baranson, J.
*North-South Technology Transfer; Financing and Institution Building.* Mt. Airy, NC, Lomond Pubs., 1981, 171p.

**412**
Castellanos Guerrero, A.
*Ciudad Juarez: la Vida Fronteriza.* México, Ed. Nuestro Tiempo, 1981, 225p.

**413**

Cleary, Amity
*A Comparative Analysis of Occupational Health and Safety Issues in the Electronic Industry: Silicon Valley, California, and Ciudad Juarez, Mexico.* (Master's thesis, Latin American Studies, University of California-Santa Cruz), 1981.

**414**

Duffy, Michael K., & Ladman, J.
*The Simultaneous Determination of Income and Employment in the United States-Mexico Border Region Economies.* Alexandria, VA (Institute of Naval Studies, Center for Naval Analyses, 2000 N. Beauregard St., Alexandria, VA 22311), 1981, 32 & 5pp.

**415**

*La Frontera del Norte: Integración y Desarrollo.* México, El Colegio de México, 1981, 366p.

**415-A**

Garreau, Joel
*The Nine Nations of North America.* Boston: Houghton Mifflin, 1981, 427p. (see chapter entitled "Mexamerica," pp. 207-244).

**416**

Gambrill, Monica C.
"Commentarios a la Ponencia Empleo vía Maquiladoras: el Caso de Tijuana." Paper at Primer Encuentro Sobre Impactos Regionales de las Relaciones Económicas México-Estados Unidos, Guanajuato, Gtq., 7-11 de julio, 1981.

**417**

Gomez-Robledo Verduzco, A., ed.
*Relaciones México-Estados Unidos: una Visión Interdisciplinaria.* México, Universidad Nacional Autónoma de México, 1981, 438p.

**418**
Gonzalez Salazar, R., comp.
*La Frontera del Norte: Integración y Desarrollo*. México, El Colegio de México, 1981, 366p.

**419**
Hansen, Niles
*The Border Economy: Regional Development in the Southwest*. Austin, University of Texas Press, 1981, 225p.

**420**
Heyman, T., & León y Ponce de León, A.
*La Inversión en México*. México, Universidad del Valle de México, 1981, 285p.

**421**
*Mexico and the United States: Energy, Trade, Investment, Immigration, Tourism; the American Assembly*. Ed. by Robert J. McBride. Englewood Cliffs, NJ, Prentice-Hall, 1981, 197p.

**422**
México. Secretaría de Programación y Presupuesto
*Estadística de la Industria Maquiladora de Exportacion, 1974-1980*. México, 1981.

**423**
Riquelme, Carlos
"Personnel Requirements for the In-Bond Industry in Mexico: Current Status and Prospects." Paper presented at seminar: Mexico's Maquiladora (In-Bond Assembly) Industry: Current Status and Prospects for Evolution. Guadalajara, American Chamber of Commerce of Mexico in Guadalajara, Jalisco, México, April 1-3, 1981.

**424**
Seligson, Mitchell A., & Williams, Edward J.
*Maquiladoras and Migration: Workers in the Mexico-United States Border Industrialization Program*. Austin, Mexico-U.S. Research Program, University of Texas; distributed by the University of Texas Press, 1981, 202p.

**425**
Evans, Peter B., & Goreffi, Gary
"Transnational Corporations, Dependent Development and State Policy in the Semiperiphery: A Comparison of Brazil and Mexico." *Latin American Research Review* (16: 3), 1981, pp. 31-64.

**426**
Miller, Tom
*On the Border: Portraits of America's Southwestern Frontier.* New York, Harper & Row, 1981, 226p.

**427**
Rivera, Julius, & Goodman, Paul W.
"System-Environment Adaptations: Corporations in a U.S.-Mexico Border Metropolis." *Studies in Comparative International Development* (16: 2), 1981, pp. 24-46.

**428**
Van Waas, Michael
*The Multinationals' Strategy for Labor; Foreign Assembly Plants in Mexico's Border Industrialization Program.* Stanford, CA: 1981, 409p. (Ph.D. Dissertation, Stanford University)

**429**
Tótoro Nieto, D.
"Reflexiones Sobre los Objetivos del Desarrollo Industrial de México en los Ochenta." México, *Comercio Exterior* (31: 8), 1981, pp. 889-894.

**429-A**
Westphalen, Jürgen
"Investitionsland der Zukunft?" Cologne, Germany: *Die Bank* 1, 1981, pp. 35-37.

**430**
Alarcón Inglesias, Norma Rafael
"Los Standars de Producción." México, *Boletín Informativo Sobre Asuntos Migratorios y Fronterizos* #15, Comité de Servicio de los Amigos, January-February 1981, pp. 6-7.

**431**
"Maquiladora Clandestina en Tijuana Cerró sus Puertas." México, *Boletín Informativo Sobre Asuntos Migratorios y Fronterizos* 15, January-February 1981, p. 8.

**432**
Coppock, Shelley
"Movimiento de Huelga en Maquiladoras de Tijuana." México, *Boletín Informativo Sobre Asuntos Migratorios y Fronterizos.* Comité de Servicio de los Amigos #16, March-April 1981, pp. 6-7.

**433**
"The Máquila Woman." Denver, CO, *Big Mama Rag* (9: 4), April 1981, p. 15.

**434**
Bennett, Douglas C., & Sharpe, Kenneth A.
"El Control Sobre las Multinacionales: las Contradicciones de la Mexicanización." México, *Foro Internacional* 21, April-June 1981, pp. 388-427.

**435**
McGuire, S.
"Setting up Shop Down Mexico way (Plants Just Across the Border)." *Newsweek* 97, May 18, 1981, p. 96.

**436**
"1981: the In-Bond Industry Stands Firm." Mexico: *Economic Panorama* (Banco de Comercio) 31, May 1981, pp. 117-137; June 1981, pp. 149-158.

**437**
Goodman, Paul W., & Rivera, Julius
"Environment Adaptations: Corporations in a U.S.-Mexico Metropolis." *Studies in Comparative International Development* (16: 2), Summer 1981, pp. 24-46.

**438**

Hansen, Niles

"Mexico's Border Industry and the International Division of Labor." *The Annals of Regional Science* (15: 2), July 1981, pp. 1-12.

**438-A**

Montes de Oca, Rosa E., & Escudero Columna, Gerardo

"Las Empresas Transnacionales en la Industria Alimentaria Mexicana." México: *Comercio Exterior* (31: 9), 1981, pp. 986-1009. (Note: this article contains a list of 122 international-level food producers, together with their Mexican subsidiaries.)

**439**

"Transnacionales en la Frontera Norte de México." México, *Boletín Informativo Sobre Asuntos Migratorios y Fronterizos* 19, September-October 1981, pp. 6-8.

**440**

Arraus, L. M.

"La Sub-Contratación Internacional y los Países Sub-Desarrollados." San José, C.R., *Estudios Sociales Centroamericanos* 10, September-December 1981, pp. 49-83.

**441**

Ramírez de la O., Rogelio

"Las Empresas Transnacionales y el Comercio Exterior de México." México, *Comercio Exterior* (31: 10), October 1981, pp. 1154-1168.

**442**

Baerressen, D. W.

"Mexico's Assembly Program. Implications for the United States." *Texas Business Review* (55: 6), November-December 1981, pp. 253-257.

**443**

Gambrill, Monica C.

"Empleo via Maquiladoras: el Caso de Tijuana." México,

*Boletín Informativo Sobre Asuntos Migratorios y Fronterizos* 20, November-December 1981, pp. 7-9.

**444**

Chase, L.
"California's Twin Cities." *California Journal* (12: 12), December 1981, pp. 433-434.

**445**

"Border Zone Between Gulf of Mexico and Pacific Coastline Viewed." *Los Angeles Times*, December 13, 1981, section 7, p. 40, column 1.

## 1982

**446**

Fernandez Kelly, María F.
"A Comparative Study of Health-Related Issues Among Women Factory Workers in Asia and the U.S.-Mexican Border." (Paper delivered at the Meeting of the Society for the Study of Social Problems, 1982.)

**447**

House, John W.
*Frontier on the Rio Grande: A Political Geography of Development and Social Deprivation*. Oxford, England, Clarendon Press, 1982, 281p.

**448**

Aviel, D., & Aviel, J. A.
"American Investment in Mexico." Wiesbaden, Germany, *Management International Review* (22: 1), 1982, pp. 83-96.

**449**

Suarez-Villa, Luis
"Factor Utilization in Mexico's Border Industrialization Program." *Annals of Regional Science* 16, 1982, pp. 48-56.

**450**
Suarez Villa, Luis
"La Utilizacion de Factores en la Industria Maquiladora de México." Mexico: *Comercio Exterior* (32: 10), 1982, pp. 1129-1132.

**451**
Fuentes, A.
"Garment Workers Hold out on the Border (Mexican Women Await Back pay for Jobs With Bankrupt American Firm, Acapulco Fashion, in Ciudad Juarez)." *Ms.* 10, January 1982, p. 19.

**452**
Peñaloza, T.
"Un Esquema para la Promoción de Manufacturas en México." México, *Trimestre Económico* (49: 1), January-March 1982, pp. 81-103.

**453**
Press, Robert M.
"U.S. Investment Brings new Factories, Technology, and jobs to Mexico: Long-Term Prospect is Less Migration North of the Border—but Will the Shift of American Factories Hurt U.S. Workers?" *Christian Science Monitor*, February 2, 1982, p. 1, column 1.

**453-A**
Ehrke, Michael
"Internationalisierte Produktion in Mexiko." Bonn, Germany, *Vierteljahresberichte: Probleme der Entwicklungsländer*, March 1982, pp. 53-69.

**454**
Mendez, R.
"Mexicanas Challenge Oppression." New York, *Guardian* (34: 22), March 3, 1982, p. 10.

**455**
"U.S. Computer Makers Rush to set up Plants." *Business Week*, May 17, 1982, p. 45.

**456**

"Samuelson Column on U.S. Industrial Operations in Foreign Countries." *Los Angeles Times*, May 26, 1982, section 2, p. 7, column 4.

**457**

Peach, J., & Nowotny, K.
"Economic Development in Border Areas: the Case of New Mexico and Chihuahua." *Journal of Economic Issues* 16, June 1982, pp. 489-496.

**458**

Cabral, A.
"Mexicans Battle U.S. Companies." New York, *Guardian* (34: 39), June 30, 1982, p. 15.

**459**

"Mexico: a Job-Creation Drive Loses its Traction." *Business Week*, July 26, 1982, p. 32.

**460**

Stuart, A.
"Opportunity Knocks in Troubled Mexico: U.S. Companies Keep Investing in new Ventures, Counting on Tough Austerity Measures to Bring an Economic Revival." *Fortune* 106, August 23, 1982, pp. 156-158.

**461**

Fernandez, M.
"Maquiladoras." Rome, *Isis* 24, September 1982, p. 20.

**462**

"Multinational Corporation/Labor Supply." Eugene, OR, *Insurgent Sociologist* (11: 3), Fall 1982, p. 49.

**463**

"Meeting of Ten Mexican-U.S. Border Governors Begins." *Los Angeles Times*, September 20, 1982, section 4, p. 1, column 1.

**464**

Van Waas, Michael
"Multinational Corporations and the Politics of Labor Supply."
*The Insurgent Sociologist* (11: 3), Fall 1982, pp. 49-57.

**464-A**

Hugo, Klaus
"Regionalentwicklung und Raumordnungspolitik in Mexiko."
Cologne, Germany, *Raumforsch und Raumordnung* (40: 4),
1982, pp. 146-160.

**465**

"Impact of U.S.-Owned Factories on Mexican Economy Discussed." *Los Angeles Times*, September 27, 1982, section 1, p.
1, column 3.

**465-A**

Alvarez Soberanis, Jaime
"La Nueva Ley Sobre Transferencia de Tecnología: Aciertos y
Limitaciones de la Política Gubernamental." México: *Comercio
Exterior* (32: 10), 1982, pp. 1117-1124.

**466**

"Labor Unions Post Strike Notes in Key Industries Across Mexico." *Los Angeles Times*, October 21, 1982, section 1, p. 7,
column 4.

**467**

"Commercial and Residential Projects in Tijuana, Mexico, Discussed." *Los Angeles Times*, November 14, 1982, section 7, p.
1, column 5.

## *1983*

**468**

Fernandez Kelly, Maria P.
*For we are Sold, I and my People: Women and Industry in Mexico's Frontier*. Albany, State University of New York Press,
1983, 217p.

**469**
Martínez, Oscar J.
*The Foreign Orientation of the Mexican Border Economy*. El Paso, Center for Inter-American and Border Studies, University of Texas at El Paso, 1983, 19p.

**470**
Tamayo, Jesús, & Fernandez, José L.
*Zonas Fronterizas (México-Estados Unidos)*. México, Centro de Investigación y Docencia Económicas, A.C., 1983, 231p.

**471**
U.S. House. Committee on Government Operations. Commerce, Consumer & Monetary Affairs Subcommittees
*Impact of Peso Devaluations on U.S. Small Business and Adequate of SBA's Peso Pack Program: Hearing, May 20, 1983*. 98th Congress, 1st Session. Washington, 1983, 609p.

**472**
Dillman, C. D.
"Assembly Industries in Mexico: Contents of Development." *Journal of Interamerican Studies and World Affairs* (25: 1), 1983, pp. 31-58.

**472-A**
Garza, Gustavo
"Desarrollo conómico, Urbanización, y Políticas Urbano-Regionales en México (1900-1982)." México, *Demografia y Economia* (17:2), 1983, pp. 157-180.

**473**
Grunwald, Joseph
"Restructuración de la Industria Maquiladora." México, *Trimestre Económico* (50: 4), 1983, pp. 2123-2150.

**474**
Martínez del Campo, Manuel
"Ventajas e Inconvenientes de la Actividad Maquiladora en México: Algunos Aspectos de la Subcontratación Internacional." México, *Comercio Exterior* (33: 2), 1983, pp. 146-151.

**474-A**
Hernandez Laos, Enrique
"Productividad y Desarrollo Industrial en México." México, *Comercio Exterior* (33: 8), 1983, pp. 679-688.

**475**
Suarez-Villa, Luis
"El Ciclo del Proceso de Manufactura y la Industrialización de las Zonas Fronterizas de México y Estados Unidos." México, *Comercio Exterior* (33: 10), 1983, pp. 950-960.

**476**
Tiano, Susan B., & Arriola Woog, Mario
"El Programa Mexicano de Maquiladoras: una Respuesta a las Necesidades de la Industria Norteamericana." *Aztlan* (14: 1), 1983, pp. 201-208.

**477**
Seligson, Mitchell A., & Williams, Edward J.
"U.S.-Mexico Border Industry is Boon: Program Benefits Both Countries, Signifies Important tie." *Los Angeles Times*, January 20, 1983, section II, p. 11, column 3.

**478**
Turner, R.
"Mexico Seminar Responds to Commercial Issues Facing U.S. Suppliers and Investors in Mexico." *Business America* 6, March 7, 1983, pp. 14-15.

**479**
Starr, M.
"The Border: a World Apart." *Newsweek* 101, April 11, 1983, pp. 36-40.

**480**
Diehl, P. N.
"The Effects of the Peso Devaluation on Texas Border Cities." *Texas Business Review* 57, May-June 1983, pp. 120-125.

**481**
Mack, T.
"Constructive Criticism (U.S.-Owned Factories on the Mexican Border)." *Forbes* 131, May 23, 1983, p. 50.

**482**
Blomström, M., & Persson, H.
"Foreign Investment and Spillover Efficiency in an Underdeveloped Economy: Evidence From the Mexican Manufacturing Industry." *World Development* 11, June 1983, pp. 493-501.

**483**
"Why Apple Wants a Mexican Branch." *Business Week*, June 13, 1983, p. 51.

**484**
"Feminists Organize in Tijuana." San Diego, *Longest Revolution* (7: 6), August 1983, p. 1.

**485**
"Meeting with President Miguel de la Madrid Hurtado of Mexico . . ." *Weekly Compilation of Presidential Documents* 19, August 22, 1983, pp. 1134-1142.

**486**
Grunwald, Joseph
"Restructuración de la Industria Maquiladora." México, *Trimestre Económico* (L: 4, #200), October-December 1983, pp. 2123-2152.

**487**
Ikonicoff, Moisés
"Las dos Etapas de la Industrialización del Tercer Mundo." México, *Trimestre Económico* (L: 4, #200), October-December 1983, pp. 2153-2172.

**488**
Hansen, Niles
"Interdependence Along the U.S.-Mexican Border." *Texas*

*Business Review* (57: 6), November-December 1983, pp. 249-254.

**489**
"U.S. Computer Makers are Feeling at Home." *Business Week*, November 14, 1983, p. 64.

**490**
Turner, R.
"Mexico Turns to its In-Bond Industry as a Means of Generating Exchange." *Business America* (6: 24), November 28, 1983, pp. 27-33.

**491**
"Ford Announces Proposal to Build Assembly Plant in Mexico." *Los Angeles Times*, December 3, 1983, section 4, p. 1, column 2.

## *1984*

**492**
"Sixty Cents an Hour." *Sixty Minutes* (Television Program), Volume XVII, No. 4, as Broadcast over the CBS Television Network, Sunday, October 7, 1984, 7-8 p.m., Eastern Daylight Time. With CBS News Correspondents Mike Wallace, Morley Safer, Harry Reasoner and Ed Bradley. "Sixty Cents an Hour" produced by Marti Galovic Palmer. New York: CBS News, 1984. (script)

**493**
Tiano, Susan B.
*Maquiladoras, Women's Work and Unemployment in Northern Mexico*. East Lansing, MI, Office of Women in International Development, Center for International Development, Michigan State University, 1984, 32p.

**494**
Del Castillo, R. G.
"New Perspectives on the Mexican and American Borderlands." *Latin American Research Review* (19: 1), 1984, pp. 199-209.

**494-A**
Brambila, Carlos, & Salazar, Héctor
*"Concentración y Distribución de los Tamaños de Ciudades en México, 1940 a 1980."* México, *Demografía y Economía* (18: 1), 1984, pp. 48-85.

**494-B**
Graizbord, Boris
"Desarrollo Regional, Ciudades Intermedias y Descentralización en México: Observaciones Críticas al Plan National de Desarrollo Urbano." México, *Demografía y Economía* (18: 1), 1984, pp. 27-47.

**494-C**
Warman, José
"Marcos de Referencia y Opciones de Política para el Desarrollo de la Industria Electrónica en México." México, *Comercio Exterior* (34: 1), 1984, pp. 67-76.

**495**
Herzog, Lawrence A.
"Prelude to a Binational Planning Model: a Portrait of Land Development Decisions in the California Border Region." *New Scholar* (9: 1-2), 1984, pp. 153-170.

**496**
Nalven, Joseph
"A Cooperation Paradox and a 'Airy Tale' Along the Border." *New Scholar* (9: 1-2), 1984, pp. 171-179.

**497**
Pinera Ramírez, David, & Saxod, Elsa
"Border Communities as a Field of Historical Investigation." *New Scholar* (9: 1-2), 1984, pp. 135-141.

**498**
Seligson, Mitchell A. et al.
"Maquiladoras and Migration." *Migration Review* (18: 2), 1984, pp. 328-329. (book review)

**499**

Stoddard, Elwyn R.

"Northern Mexican Migration and the U.S.-Mexico Border Region." *New Scholar* (9: 1-2), 1984, pp. 51-72.

**500**

Young, Gay

"Women, Development and Human Rights: Issues in Integrated Transnational Production." *The Journal of Applied Behavioral Science* (20: 4), 1984, pp. 383-401.

**501**

Unger, Kurt

"El Comercio Exterior de Manufacturas en México (1977-1983)." México, *Economía de América Latina* 11, First Semester, 1984, pp. 185-196.

**502**

Suarez-Villa, Luis

"The Manufacturing Process Cycle and the Industrialization of the United States-Mexico Borderlands." *Annals of Regional Science* 18, March 1984, pp. 1-23.

**503**

"What Made Apple Seek Safety in Numbers." *Business Week*, March 12, 1984, p. 42.

**504**

Meislin, Richard J.

"Mexican Border Plants Beginning to Hire men; job Growth Aids Women." *New York Times*, March 19, 1984, pp. 32-N, D8(L), column 1.

**505**

Carrillo Viveros, Jorge

"La Crisis y el Movimiento Obrero en la Frontera Norte de México." *The Borderlands Journal* (7: 2), Spring 1984, pp. 127-147.

**506**
"México: Programa Nacional de Fomento Industrial y Comercio Exterior, 1984-1988." México, *Economía de América Latina* 12, Second Semester, 1984, pp. 189-210.

**507**
Rosenfeldt, Martin E., & Halatin, T.
"Marketing Strategies in a Changing Environment: Emphasis on U.S.-Mexican Borderland Businesses." *Business & Society* 23, Spring 1984, pp. 45-51.

**508**
Russell, J. W.
"A Borderline Case." *The Progressive* 48, April 1984, pp. 34-37.

**509**
Fernandez Kelly, María P.
"Mujeres y Maquiladoras en Ciudad Juarez." México: *Cuadernos Politicos* 40, April-June 1984, pp. 80-100.

**510**
Dávila, Alberto E. et al.
"Industrial Diversification, Exchange Rate Shocks, and the Texas-Mexico Border." *Federal Reserve Bank of Dallas*, May 1984, pp. 1-9.

**511**
Lee, Cecil G.
"Honeywell Likes Mexico." Minneapolis, *Northern Sun News* (7: 4), May 1984, p. 9.

**512**
Dahlman, C. J., & Cortés, M.
"Mexico (Technological Exports)." *World Development* 12, May-June 1984, pp. 601-624.

**513**
Miller, Marjorie
"Boom Times for Border Town job Market; Foreign-Owned

Plants in Scarmble for Assembly Line Workers in Mexico." *Los Angeles Times*, May 14, 1984, section II, p. 1, column 1.

**514**
Brill, J.
"Will Mexico's Welcome Last?" Marion, OH, *The Nation* (38: 19), May 19, 1984, p. 602.

**515**
"Méxique: de Nouvelles Perspectives pour les Investissements Étrangers." Paris, *Industries et Travaux d'Outremer* 32, June 1984, pp. 336-339.

**516**
Blanco, Iris, & Solórzano, Rosario
"O te Aclimatas o te Aclimueres: la Mujer Invisible: Aspectos de la Emigración en la Frontera con California." México, *Fem* 34, June-July 1984, pp. 20-22.

**517**
Russell, J. W.
"U.S. Sweatshops Across the Rio Grande." *Business and Society Review* 50, Summer 1984, pp. 17-20.

**518**
"Fabricating in the Far East? Mexicana Airlines Says There's a Cheaper Way." *American Import/Export Management* 101, July 1984, p. 30.

**519**
"Why an IBM Plant is Stalled at the Border." *Business Week*, August 6, 1984, p. 35.

**520**
Bustamante, Jorge A.
Migración Interna e Internacional, y Distribución del Ingreso: la Frontera Norte de México." México, *Comercio Exterior* (34: 9), September 1984, pp. 849-863.

**520-A**
Ramírez de la O., Rogelio
"L'Influence des Entreprises Transnationales sur la Balance des Paiements du Méxique." Aubervilliers Cedex, France: *Notes et Études Documentaires* #4764, 3rd quarter 1984, pp. 90-104.

**521**
Koepp, S.
"Hands Across the Border (American Manufacturers)." *Time* 124, September 10, 1984, p. 36.

**522**
Christman, John H.
"Maquiladoras: Profit From Production Sharing: Offshore Assembly Benefits Both Mexico and the U.S." *Wall Street Journal*, September 24, 1984, p. 30-W, column 4.

**523**
"Cheap Mexican Labor Spurs Border Factories." *Milwaukee Journal*, "Business" section, October 14, 1984, p. 10.

**523-A**
Unger, Kurt
"Transferencia Tecnológica y Organización Industrial en México: el Papel de las Marcas." México, *Comercio Exterior* (34: 12), 1984, pp. 1201-1206.

**524**
Field, A. M.
"The Odd Couple of the Southwest." *Business Week* 2875, December 31, 1984, p. 32-D.

*1985*

**525**
Bennett, Douglas C., & Sharpe, Kenneth A.
*Transnational Corporations vs. the State: the Political Economy of the Mexican Auto Industry*. Princeton, NJ, Princeton University Press, 1985, 300p.

**526**
George, Edward T., & Tollen, Robert D.
*The Economic Impact of the Mexican Border Industrialization Program*. El Paso, Center for Inter-American and Border Studies, University of Texas at El Paso, 1985, 27p.

**527**
Gibson, James L., & Corona Rentería, Alfonso
*The United States and Mexico: Borderland Development and the National Economies*. Boulder, CO, Westview Press, 1985, 262p.

**528**
Martínez del Campo, Manuel
*Industrialización en México: Hacia un Análisis Crítico*. México, El Colegio de México, 1985, 493p.

**529**
Musgrave, Peggy B., ed.
*Mexico and the United States: Studies in Economic Interaction*. Boulder, CO, Westview Press, 1985, 261p.

**530**
Rosenfeldt, Martin E.
"U.S.-Mexico Borderland Industrialization Policies Revisited: the Need for Binational Strategies." *Akron Business & Economic Review* 16, Winter 1985, pp. 12-19.

**531**
Tiano, Susan B.
*Export Processing, Women's Work and the Employment Problem in Developing Countries: the Maquiladora Program in Northern Mexico*. El Paso, Center for Inter-American and Border Studies, University of Texas at El Paso, 1985, 32p.

**532**
Trabis, Roland
*Industrie et Politique à la Frontière Méxique-U.S.A.: le cas de Nuevo Lardeo, 1966-1984*. Toulouse, France: Centre Nationale

de la Recherche Scientifique, Centre Régionale de Publications de Toulouse, Amérique Latine et Pays Ibériques, 1985, 241p.

**533**
U.S. Dept. of Commerce. International Trade Administration *Investing in Mexico*, by Betsy Stillman. Washington, GPO, December 1985, 20p. (Overseas Business Reports, OBR-85-19. Supt. of Documents No. C 57.11:85-19. Stock no. 803-007-00019-5.)

**534**
Bowen, R. E., & Hennessey, T. M.
"Adjacent State Issues for the United States in Establishing an Exclusive Economic Zone: the Cases of Canada and Mexico." *Ocean Development & International Law* (15: 3-4), 1985, pp. 355-375.

**535**
"IBM Wants to Build Mexican Plant." *Dun's Business Month* 125, January 1985, p. 31.

**535-A**
"Mexico Woos Foreign Investors — and Rejects Them." *Economist* 9, February 1985, pp. 49-50.

**536**
Prock, J.
"Mexico's Monetary Changes and Border Banks: an Impact Survey." *Inter-American Economic Affairs* 39, Winter 1985, pp. 71-78.

**537**
Rosenfeldt, Martin E.
"United States-Mexico Borderland Industrialization Policies Revisited: the Need for Binational Strategies." *Akron Business & Economic Review* 16, Winter 1985, pp. 12-19.

**538**
Anderson, Joan B., & Frantz, Roger S.
"Production Efficiency Among Mexican Apparel Assembly

Plants." *Journal of Developing Areas* 19, April 1985, pp. 369-378.

**539**
Nelson, C. A.
"Manufacturing in Mexico Using a Maquiladora." *American Import/Export Management* 102, April 1985, p. 66.

**540**
Reynolds, Clark W.
"Modeling U.S.-Mexico Economic Linkages." *American Economic Review* 75, May 1985, pp. 217-222.

**540-A**
Unger, Kurt
"El Comercio Exterior de Manufacturas Modernas en México: el Papel de las Empresas Extranjeras." México, *Comercio Exterior* (35: 5), 1985, pp. 431-443.

**541**
Moffett, Matt
"Area Along Border of Mexico, U.S. has a Culture all its own; Biggest Industry in Region is Illegal Immigration; how to Speak Spanglish; Juarez's Wading Commuters." *Wall Street Journal* May 3, 1985, pp. 1-E, 1-W, column 6.

**542**
Orme, William A., Jr.
"Maquiladoras Thrive on Mexican Border." *Journal of Commerce and Commercial* 364, May 8, 1985, p. 4-A.

**543**
Kramer, M.
"U.S.-Mexican Border: Life on the Line." *National Geographic* 167, June 1985, pp. 720-749.

**544**
Van der Spak, G.
"Mexico's Booming Border Zone: a Magnet for Labor-Intensive

American Plants." *Inter-American Economic Affairs* 29, Summer 1985, pp. 33-47.

**545**
Herzog, Lawrence A.
"The Cross-Cultural Dimensions of Urban Land use Policy on the U.S.-Mexican Border: a San Diego-Tijuana Case Study." Fort Worth, TX, *Social Science Journal* 22, July 1985, pp. 29-46.

**546**
Hill, J. K.
"The Economic Impact of Tighter U.S. Border Security." *Federal Reserve Bank of Dallas Economic Review*, July 1985, pp. 12-20.

**546-A**
Wuffli, Peter A.
"Wandel der Mexikanischen Politik gegenüber Auslandsinvestitionen? die 'Irrationale' Komponente der Mexikanisierungsstrategie." St. Gail, Switzerland: *Aussenwirt* (40: 3), 1985, pp. 229-254.

**547**
Lineback, J. R.
"Computer Maker Heads South of the Border for new Markets; Hopes run High That Mexico Will Loosen Controls, Providing Future Entry into Latin America." *Electronics Week* 58, July 8, 1985, pp. 28-29.

**548**
Magnuson, E.
"Symbiosis Along 1,936 Miles." *Time* 126, July 8, 1985, pp. 54-55.

**549**
Cook, B.
"Mexico (GE Company)." *Electronic Business* 11, July 15, 1985, p. 182.

**550**
Wyeth, S.
"Mexico's Maquiladoras: in-Bond Assembly Attracts Foreign Investment." Atlanta, *Site Selection Handbook* 30 (Conway Associates), August 1985, pp. 54-56.

**551**
Lenckus, Dave
"Competition Forces Improvements in Mexican Furniture Operation (Maquila Program) (the Major Players)." *Wood and Wood Products* 90, September 1985, pp. 58-62.

**552**
Beane, S. R.
"Maquiladoras Pose Special Problems." *Business Insurance* 19, October 7, 1985, p. 30.

**553**
Harrell, L., & Fischer, D.
"The 1982 Mexican Peso Devaluation and Border Area Development." *Monthly Labor Review* 108, October 1985, pp. 25-32.

**554**
Rivas, F., Sergio
"La Industria Maquiladora en México: Realidades y Falacias." México, *Comercio Exterior* (35: 11), 1985, pp. 1071-1084.

**555**
Urquidi, Victor L., & Carrillo, Mario M.
"Desarrollo Económico e Interacción en la Frontera Norte de México." México: *Comercio Exterior* (35: 11), 1985, pp. 1060-1070.

**556**
Herzog, Lawrence A.
"Tijuana." *Cities* 2, November 1985, pp. 297-306.

**557**
Freiwald, A.
"Mexico: a Multinational Haven." Washington, *Multinational Monitor* (6: 16), November 15, 1985, p. 1.

**558**
Walsh, Mary (Williams)
"Mexican Factories Along the U.S. Border Succeed Despite Criticism on Both Sides." *Wall Street Journal*, November 19, 1985, pp. 35-E, 39-W.

*1986*

**558-A**
Alvarez Lopez, Juan, & Castillo, Víctor, M.
*Ecología y Frontera*. México, Escuela de Economía, Universidad Autónoma de Baja California, 1986, 258p.

**558-B**
*El Capital Extranjero en México*. México, Ed. Nuestro Tiempo, 1986, 253p.

**559**
Herzog, Lawrence A., ed.
*Planning the International Border Metropolis: Trans-Boundary Policy Options for the San Diego-Tijuana Region*. La Jolla, CA, Center for U.S.-Mexican Studies, University of California, San Diego, 1986, 108p.

**559-A**
Hiernaux, Daniel
*Urbanización y Autoconstrucción de Vivienda en Tijuana*. México, Centro de Ecodesarrollo, 1986, 146p.

**559-B**
Margulis, Mario, & Tuirán, Rodolfo
*Desarrollo y Población en la Frontera Norte: el Caso de Reynosa*. México: El Colegio de México, Centro de Estudios Demográficos y de Desarrollo Urbano, 1986, 323p.

**560**
Martínez, Oscar J., ed.
*Across Boundaries; Transborder Interaction in Comparative Perspective*. El Paso, TX: Texas Western Press, 1986, 206p.

**560-A**
México. Instituto Nacional de Estadística, Geografía e Informática
*Estadística de la Industria Maquiladora de Exportación, 1975-1984*. México, 1986, 47 + 2pp.

**561**
Weisman, Alan
*La Frontera; the United States Border With Mexico*. Photographs by Jay Dusard. San Diego, CA, Harcourt Brace Jovanovich, 1986, 200p.

**562**
Young, Gay, ed.
*The Social Ecology and Economic Development of Ciudad Juarez*. Boulder, CO, Westview Press, 1986, 171p.

**563**
Carrillo Viveros, Jorge
"Conflictos Laborales en la Industria Maquiladora de Exportación." México: *Comercio Exterior* (36: 1), 1986, pp. 46-57.

**564**
Conkling, E.
"Made in USA/Mexico: a new Industrial Partnership." *Focus* 36, Winter 1986, pp. 32-33.

**565**
"Mexico's Maquiladoras Examined: are In-Bond Production Plants the Wave of the Future?" *Pepperdine Legal Review*, January 1986, pp. 357-385.

**565-A**
Negrete Salas, María E., & Salazar Sanchez, Héctor
"Zonas Metropolitanas en México, 1980." México, *Estudios Demográficos y Urbanos* (1: 1), 1986, pp. 97-124.

**566**

Weston, Scott N.

"United States-Mexico: Coping with Environmental Problems at the Border." *Loyola of Los Angeles International & Comparative Law Journal* (9: 1), 1986, pp. 117-136.

**567**

Gettman, D., & Peña, Devon G.

"Women, Mental Health and the Workplace in a Transnational Setting." *Social Work* 31, January-February 1986, pp. 5-11.

**568**

"Mexican Government now Views 'Maquiladoras' Foreign-Owned Factories, Mostly American, that are Located in Mexico, as key Part of Country's Plan to Rebuild its Economy . . ." *New York Times*, January 19, 1986, sec. III, p. 4, column 3.

**569**

Stockton, William

"Mexico's Grand 'Maquiladora' Plan; the Government has Eased the Rules Hoping for an Economic Lift." *New York Times*, January 19, 1986, section 3, pp. F4(N), F4(L).

**570**

Gowens, P.

"Woman to Woman in Mexico." Washington: *Off Our Backs* (16: 3), March 1986, p. 3.

**570-A**

Humbert, Marc

"L'Électronique dans le Politique Industrielle Méxicaine." Aubervilliers Cedex, France: *Notes et Études Documentaires* (serie: Problèmes Amérique Latines), 2d quarter 1986, pp. 67-92.

**571**

Johnston, C.

"When Earth Trembled in Mexico/Women's Working Conditions." Englewood, NJ, *New Directions for Women* (15: 2), March 1986, p. 1.

**572**

"Awkward Neighbors." *The Economist* 299, April 5, 1986, pp. 11-12.

**573**

"El Norte." *The Economist* 299, April 5, 1986, p. 22.

**574**

Auerbach, Stuart
   "Mexican Border Towns Boom; $1.30-an-Hour Wages Attract U.S. Companies." *Washington Post*, April 20, 1986, p. F-1, column 4.

**575**

Rivera-Batiz, F. L.
   "Can Border Industries be a Substitute for Immigration?" *The American Economic Review* 76, May 1986, pp. 263-268.

**576**

White, Charles A.
   "Hands Across Two Borders." Toronto: *Canada & World* 51, May 1986, p. 8.

**577**

"Commentary on Americanization of Northern Areas Threatening Rule by PRI Party in Upcoming State Elections." *Washington Post*, May 25, 1986, section C, p. 1, column C.

**578**

Callahan, J. M.
   "Mexico's Hidden Treasure: the Magical Maquiladoras." *Automotive Industries* 166, June 1986, pp. 87-88.

**579**

Reifenberg, S.
   "Contract Assembly on the Mexican Border (Maquiladoras)." *Electronic Business* 12, July 1, 1986, pp. 114-116.

**580**
Gomez, L.
"Borderland: Between Texas and Mexico, a River and a Troublesome Future." *Life* 9, August 1986, pp. 40-48.

**581**
"Suddenly it's Mexico." *The Economist* 300, August 9, 1986, pp. 17-18.

**582**
O'Reilly, B.
"Business Makes a run for the Border." *Fortune* 114, August 18, 1986, pp. 70-76.

**582-A**
Blomström, M.
"Multinationals and Market Structure in Mexico." Oxford, England, *Journal of Industrial Economics* 35, September 1986, pp. 97-110.

**583**
*One River, One Country: the U.S./Mexico Border* (videotape). Elena Mannes, Director. Elena Mannes and Bill Moyers, Writers. Reported by Bill Moyers. CBS Reports Series. Televised on the CBS Television Network, September 3, 1986, 7:00-8:00 PM, Central Daylight Time. New York: Columbia Broadcasting System. 1986 (in color).

**584**
*Global Assembly Line (the International Search for Low-Wage Labor)* (videotape). Lorraine Gray, Director. Mary Lampson and Sara Fishko, Editors. Televised by TV Channel 36, Milwaukee, WI, September 6, 1986, 8:00-9:00 PM, Central Daylight Time. Washington: Educational TV & Film Center, Public Broadcasting System, 1986 (in black and white).

**585**
Fernandez Kelly, María P.
"International Development and Women's Employment." New York: *Women's Studies Quarterly* (14: 3), Fall 1986, p. 2.

**586**
McHugh, Paul D., & Rucker, Helen, eds.
"United States-Mexico Transboundary Resource Issues." *National Resources Journal* 26, Fall 1986, pp. 661-850.

**587**
Wilson, C.
"Maquiladoras: Benefits for U.S. Manufacturers." *Business America* 9, October 13, 1986, pp. 14-15.

**588**
Finley, S.
"Profitable Tariffs: Special Customs Codes send Molders South of the Border (Offshore Manufacturing: inbond or Maquiladora Program)." *Plastics World* 44, November 1986, p. 19.

**589**
"Toshiba Moves to Mexico (TV Plant)." *TV Digest* 26, November 17, 1986, p. 12.

**590**
LaFranchi, Howard
"U.S. Firms Moving Plants to Mexico; Cheap Labor is the Pull, but U.S. Border Regions Benefit, too." *Christian Science Monitor*, December 22, 1986, p. 3.

**591**
Applebone, Peter
"U.S. Goods Made in Mexico Raise Concern in job Losses." *New York Times* 136, December 29, 1986 (National edition), section Ap, p. 1, column 2.

**592**
Murray, W.
"Twins." *New Yorker* 62, December 29, 1986, pp. 63-64.

### 1987

**592-A**
Barrerra Bassols, Dália
*Condiciones de Vida de los Trabajadores de Tijuana, 1970-*

*1978*. México: Instituto Nacional de Antropología e Historia, 1987, 142p.

**593**
Stoddard, Elwyn R.
*Máquila: Assembly Plants in Northern Mexico.* Austin: University of Texas Press, 1987, 91p.

**594**
U.S. House. Committee on Banking, Finance and Urban Affairs. Subcommittee on Economic Stabilization
*Commerce Department's Promotion of Mexico's Twin Plant Program:* Hearing before the Subcommittee on Economic Stabilization of the Committee on Banking, Finance, and Urban Affairs, House of Representatives, 99th Congress, 2d Session, November 25, 1986. Washington: GPO, for sale by the Superintendent of Documents, 1986 (i.e., 1987), 137p. (Y4.B 22/1:99-105).

**595**
"An Investor's Introduction to Mexico's Maquiladora Program." *Texas International Law Journal* 22, Winter 1987, pp. 109-139.

**596**
"Manufacturing: Mexican Plants cut Labor, Operation Costs." *Plastics World* 45, January 1987, p. 19.

**597**
Copeland, J. B.
"The Rise of Gringo Capitalism (U.S. Companies in the Border Zone)." *Newsweek* 109, January 5, 1987, pp. 40-41.

**598**
"Editorial Supports U.S. Government-Sanctioned 'Maquiladora' Program With Mexico Because it Reduces Cost of Manufactured Goods to Consumers and Shores up Mexico's Faltering Economy; Maintains That Although Pressure is Building to Limit Twin-Plant Maquiladoras or cut Them Back, Congress Would be 'Foolhardy' to Interfere." *New York Times*, January 5, 1987, section I, p. 16, column 1.

**599**

Bywater, William H., & Baumann, Elizabeth
"How U.S. and Mexican Workers Lose Together: Twin-Plant Program" (Letter to the Editor). *New York Times*, January 26, 1987, p. 20-N, p. A-34(L).

**600**

Bazzy, D.
"Made in Mexico." Washington, *Multinational Monitor* (8: 2), February 1987, p. 3.

**601**

Eason, H.
"Going South to cut Costs (U.S. Firms in Mexico)." *Nation's Business* 75, February 1987, p. 24.

**602**

Moore, Michael
"Made in Mexico: Reagan Administration Encourages U.S. Businesses to Move Jobs South of the Border." Washington, *Multinational Monitor* 8, February 1987, pp. 3-6.

**603**

Rodriguez, Richard
"Across the Borders of History." *Harpers* 274, March 1987, pp. 42-49.

**604**

Wiegner, K. K.
"How to mix Sake and Tequila (Japanese Manufacturing and Assembling in Mexico to Export to the United States)." *Forbes* 139, March 23, 1987, p. 48.

**605**

Mertens, L., & Richards, P. J.
"Recession and Employment in Mexico." Geneva, Switzerland, *International Labour Review* 126, March/April 1987, pp. 229-243.

**606**

Falcone, Angelo C.
"Mexico's in-Bond Manufacturing Program: U.S. Tax Considerations After the 1986 Tax Act; a U.S. Manufacturer may be Able to Significantly Reduce its Cost of Production by Establishing a Manufacturing Facility in Mexico Under the *Maquiladora* Program." *Taxes* 65, April 1987, pp. 211-220.

**607**

LaFranchi, Howard
"U.S. Firms Help Lighten Mexico's Debt." *Christian Science Monitor*, April 13, 1987, pp. 3, 8.

**608**

"Jack Rosenthal 'Editorial Notebook' Column: Tijuana, Mexico, and the Economic Realities That Will Continue to Push Mexicans Across Border into U.S. Even if new U.S. Immigration law Manages to Reduce the Flow." *New York Times*, April 17, 1987, section I, p. 30, column 1.

**609**

Gould, Whitney
"Assembly Plants Attracting Capital." *Milwaukee Journal*, "Accent on the News" section, May 31, 1987, p. 3-J.

**610**

"San Diego Encourages Asian Companies to Locate Assembly Plants Across Border in Mexico, Finishing Plants Near San Diego." *Los Angeles Times*, section VIII, May 31, 1987, p. 1, column 3.

**611**

Anand, V.
"Mexican Border Plants Support U.S. Trade (*Maquiladora* Plants)." *Global Trade* 106, June 1987, p. 34.

**612**

Castro, J.
"Yankee! Welcome to Mexico!" *Time* 129, June 1, 1987, p. 51.

**613**

Baker, S.
"Mexico Looks Better and Better to Japan." *Business Week*, June 8, 1987, p. 58.

**614**

U.S. House. Committee on Government Operations, Commerce, Consumer & Monetary Affairs Subcommittee
*Maquiladora Impact on U.S. Jobs and Trade Competition with Japan: Hearing, June 12, 1987*. Washington, GPO, 1987, 267p. (100th Congress, 1st session) (SD catalog no. Y 4.g 74/7: M 32)

**614-A**

"U.S. Congress to Target Mexico's in-Bond Industry in Review of Trade Schemes." *Business Latin America*, June 15, 1987, p. 190.

**615**

Lawson, M.
"New Assembly Plants Boost El Paso, Juarez (Maquiladoras)." *ENR* 218, June 18, 1987, pp. 40-41.

**616**

Stokes, Bruce
"Mexican Momentum: Mixing High Technology With Cheap Labor, U.S.-Backed Firms are Making State-of-the-Art Products at Mexican Plants and Presenting a new Challenge to the U.S. Economy." *National Journal* 19, June 20, 1987, pp. 1572-1578.

**617**

Contreras, J.
"The Far East Goes South (Japanese Factories)." *Newsweek* 109, June 22, 1987, p. 46.

**618**

"South of South-land's Border (Offshore Manufacturing Contracts From Southern California)." *Electronic Business* 13, July 1, 1987, p. 98.

**618-A**

"Seven Management Tips Mark *Maquiladora* Success of Cincinnati Electronics." *Business Latin America*, July 27, 1987, pp. 233-235.

**619**

Hawkins, S. L.
"Tokyo Opens a Southern Trade Route (Factories in Mexico)." *U.S. News & World Report* 103, August 3, 1987, p. 40.

**620**

"Trends Across the Border." New York, *Economic Notes* (55: 9), September 1987, p. 12.

**621**

Elliot, M.
"Our Friends to the North." *The Economist* 304, September 5, 1987, survey, pp. 12-15.

**622**

Bouleau, C.
"Rapid Growth Strains Mexican Border Area (*Maquiladoras*)." *Electronic News* 33, supplement, September 14, 1987, p. 9.

**623**

Hurlbert, L.
"*Maquiladoras*: Borderline Logistics in Mexico." *Distribution* 86, October 1987, pp. 50-51.

**624**

Mattel Toy Company Announces Closing of Last U.S. Plant at Paramount, California, as it Takes its Toy Production to Mexico." *Los Angeles Times*, section VIII, October 3, 1987, p. 29, column 1.

**625**

Kuzda, L.
"Production Sharing: Mexico Another Japan? Twins may be First Step (*Maquiladora* and Twin Plant Program)." *Industry Week* 235, November 2, 1987, pp. 28-29.

**626**

Pearce, J.

"Mexico Holds Special Place in Heart of Japan (Interview with S. G. Galvez, Ambassador of Mexico)." *Business Japan* 32, November-December, 1987, pp. 47-49.

**626-A**

"Feature on Economic Growth and Increasing Cultural Sophistication of Tijuana, Mexico." *Los Angeles Times*, section I, November 18, 1987, p. 1, column 1.

**626-B**

"Article on Effect of Falling Peso in Latin America, and U.S.-Mexico Border Areas, With Emphasis on Mexican Workers and Travelers." *Los Angeles Times*, section IV, November 20, 1987, p. 1, column 4.

**626-C**

"U.S. and Mexican Border State Governors set Industrialization, Economic Development Along Border as top Priority Over Drug Enforcement." *Los Angeles Times*, section I, December 12, 1987, p. 29, column 1.

**627**

Chayet, Z. V.

"An Overview of the *Maquiladora* Industry." In: *Mexico and the United States: Strengthening the Relationship. California Western International Law Journal* 18, Winter 1987-1988, pp. 1-200.

**628**

Conrow, J. W.

"Structural Reform and the Debt Strategy: the Mexican Case." In: *Mexico and the United States: Strengthening the Relationship. California Western International Law Journal* 18, Winter 1987-1988, pp. 1-200.

**629**

Gordon, M. W.

"Mexico and the United States: Common Frontier — Uncommon

Relationship." In: *Mexico and the United States: Strengthening the Relationship. California Western International Law Journal* 18, Winter 1987-1988, pp. 1-200.

**630**

Valdez, A. L.

"Strengthening the United States-Mexico Relation: a Proposal for Establishing a Free-Trade Zone and co-Production Zone." In: *Mexico and the United States: Strengthening the Relationship. California Western International Law Journal* 18, Winter 1987-1988, pp. 1-200.

**631**

Zamora, S.

"*Maquiladora* Operations. A Comment on the Maquiladora Program in Mexico." In: *Mexico and the United States: Strengthening the Relationship. California Western International Law Journal* 18, Winter 1987-1988, pp. 1-200.

**632**

Gräder, S.

"Through the 'Back Door' (Japanese Factories)." *World Press Review* 35, January 1988, p. 48.

**633**

Ehrenthal, David, & Newman, Joseph

"Explaining Mexico's *Máquila* Boom." *SAIS Review*, Winter/ Spring 1988, pp. 189-211.

**634**

Jenish, D.

"The Mexican Border Attraction (Canadian Factories in Mexico)." Toronto: *Maclean's* 101, March 14, 1988, pp. 46-47.

**635**

Bieber, Owen

"U.S. Labor and Global Manufacturing." *Vital Speeches of the Day* (LIV: 15), May 15, 1988, pp. 456-459. (speech by labor union official).

**636**

*Nine Nations of North America: Mex-America* (videotape)
Joel Garreau, interlocutor. Philip Burton, producer. Philip Burton Productions, Inc. 1987. Telecast on TV Channel 11, Chicago, IL, June 8, 1988, 10-11 PM, Central Daylight Time. (Channel 11 is the Chicago television station of the Public Broadcasting Service.)

**636-A**

*Adam Smith's Money World:* "Mexico's Crisis: A Special Report." Adam Smith, host. Alvin Perlmutter, executive producer. Larry Keith, narrator. Adrian Lajous, economic consultant. Produced by WNET and Alvin Perlmutter, Inc. Telecast over TV Channel 10, Public Broadcasting Service, Milwaukee, WI, July 3, 1988, 4:30-5:00 PM, Central Daylight Time (videotape).

# IV. Author Index

Note: all numbers refer to individual entries, and not to page numbers.

## A

*Adam Smith's Money World*, 636-A
"AFL-CIO to U.S. Government:
    Stop Encouraging Runaways",
    114
Aguilar, Juan J., 141-A
Aguilar, Alvarez, I., 130
Aguilar Montaverde, A., 281
Alarcón Iglesias, Norma Rafael, 430
Alba, F., 303
Alcalá Quintero, F., 67
"Allen Bradley Planning Mexican
    Resistor Facility", 128
Alvarez Lopez, Juan, 558-A
Alvarez Sobernais, Jaime, 465-A
Amador Leal, A., 270
"An Investor's Introduction to
    Mexico's Maquiladora Program",
    595
Anand, V., 611
Anderson, Joan B., 538
Angeles, Luis, 317-A
Applebone, Peter, 591
Arellano Rincón, S., 133
Arraus, L. M., 440
Arriola Woog, Mario, 378,476
"Article on Effect of Falling Peso in
    Latin America, and U.S.-Mexico
    Border Areas . . .", 626-B
Auerbach, Stuart, 574
Aviel, D., 448
Aviel, J. A., 448
"Awkward Neighbors", 572
Ayer, H. W., 206

## B

Baerressen, D. W., 239,442
Baird, Peter, 336
Baker, S., 613
Baranson, J., 411
Barkin, David, 146,230
Barnet, Richard J., 188
Barr, Lorna, 225
Barrera Bassols, Dália, 592-A
Barrera Bassols, J., 337
Bassols Batalla, A., 135, 338
Baumann, Elizabeth, 599
Bazzy, D., 600
Beane, S. R., 552
Bennett, Douglas C., 434,525
Berni, G., 167
Beteta, M. R., 2
Bieber, Owen, 635
"Big Companies Think Small When
    Moving Into Mexico", 1
"Big Deal at the Border", 127
Bjur, W. E., 236
Blanco, Iris, 516
Blomström, M., 482,582-A
Boatler, Robert W., 282
Bohrisch, A., 16
Bolin, Richard L., 102,183,207
Boltvinik, Julio, 292-A
Bond, M. E., 35
"Boom South of the Border Gets
    Bigger", 201
"Border Plant hit by Labor Costs",
    232

Corona Rentería, Alfonso, 527
"Corporaciones Transnacionales y
Empresas Multinacionales", 119
Cortés, M., 512
Coyle, Laurie, 341

D

Dahlman, C. J., 512
D'Antonio, William V., 4
Dávila, Alberto E., 510
"Decreto que Declara de Utilidad
Nacional . . .", 119-A
De la Rosa Hickerson, Gustavo, 342
Del Castillo, R. G., 494
"Desarrollo Regional: IV Reunión
de Trajajo para el Desarrollo
Fronterizo", 164
"Desarrollo Regional: Empresas
Maquiladoras Fronterias —
Facilidades Aduaneras y Debate
Sobre su Futuro", 84
"Desarrollo Regional: Fomento
Económico en la Frontera Norte e
Industrias Maquiladoras", 139
"Desarrollo Regional: Impulso al
Desarrollo de la Zona Fronteriza
Norte", 110
"Desarrollo Regional: los Problemas
de las Región Fronteriza Norte",
68
"Desarrollo Regional: Maquiladoras
y Comercio Fronterizo — se
Despeja el Panorama", 89
"Desarrollo Regional: PRONAF —
Respuesta al Desafío Comercial
Fronterizo", 80
"Desarrollo Regional: Prórroga del
Tratamiento Fiscal Preferencial a
la Zona Fronteriza", 111
"Desarrollo Regional: V Reunión de
Trabajo Sobre Desarrollo
Fronterizo", 180
"Desarrollo Regional: se Confirma
la Realización de Audiencias

Sobre las Industrias Fronterizas",
72
"Desarrollo Regional: VI Reunión
Nacional para el Desarrollo
Fronterizo", 208
Diehl, P. N., 480
Dillman, C. D., 18,25,57,69,74,75,
85,90,204,250,251,262,299,324,
472
Dixon, J., 304
"Doce Mil Obreras en Huelga en
Nuevo Laredo", 198
"Document Méxique", 186-A
Duffy, Michael K., 414
Duncan, C., 276

E

Eason, H., 601
Editorial Supports U.S.
Government-Sanctioned
'Maquiladora' Program . . .",
598
Ehrenthal, David, 633
Ehrke, Michael, 453-A
Elliott, M., 621
Enjalbert, H., 26
Ericson, Anna-Stina L., 17,82
Erickson, Rosemary J., 168
Escamilla, Norma, 284
Escudero Columna, Gerardo, 438-A
Evans, John S., 138,189,240
Evans, Peter B., 425

F

"Fabricating in the Far East?
Mexicana Airlines Says There's a
Cheaper Way", 518
Faesler, J., 76
Fainzylber, F., 242,252
Fairchild, Loretta, 295,305
Falcone, Angelo, 606
Farias Negrete, Jorge, 44

# V. Subject Index

Note: all numbers refer to individual entry numbers, and not to pages.

## A

Agua Príeta, Mexico/Douglas,
  Arizona, 190
Allen Bradley Company (firm), 128
Apple Computers (firm), 483, 503
Attitudes, Mexican, to
  *maquiladoras*, 1,4,60,148,364
Automobile industry, Mexico, 91,
  491,525

## B

Balance of payments, Mexican, 216,
  520-A
Border Industrialization Program
  (Mexican Government), 18,41,44,
  45,46,53,71,90,96,98,109,120,
  124,133,149,166,181,202,204,
  206-208,213,218,239,241,250,
  257,262,306,334,349,378,388,
  442,449,506,526; see also
  *Maquiladoras*
Border Studies (general), 61,141-B,
  222,226,244,260,261,276-A,285,
  288,289,294,303,309,314,315,
  322,325,335,336,345,349,350,
  355,357,387,394,415,415-A,418,
  419,421,426,446,447,470,479,
  494,496,497,508,514,532,541,
  543,558-A,559,559-B,560,561,
  568,569,576,579
Bowmar Instruments (firm), 186

Brand names (manufactured
  products), 523-A
Brownsville, Texas, 25,57

## C

Cel Mex (firm), 115
Chamizal region, U.S.-Mexico
  Border, 276-A
Chihuahua (State), Mexico,
  economic development, 457
Cities and towns (Mexican Border),
  22,85,296-A,325,494-A,494-B,
  559,559-A,559-B,560,562,626-A
Ciudad Juarez, Mexico/El Paso,
  Texas, 167,192,310,311,373,409,
  412,413,431,451,509,562
Clairol de Mexico (firm), 87
Clothing industry, Mexican Border,
  Mexican side, 397,538
Computer industry, Mexico, 455,
  489,547
Currency devaluation, Mexican,
  effect of, 471,480,510,536,553,
  626-B
Customs duties, Mexican, 103,111,
  240

## D

Demography, Mexico, see
  *Population, Mexico*

# VI. Directories

## A. BUSINESS ORGANIZATIONS

**637**

Maquiladora Services Dept., American Chamber of Commerce of Mexico, Lucerna 78, 4th Floor, México 06600, D.F., México

**638**

Cámara Nacional de la Ciudad de México (National Chamber of Commerce of Mexico City), Reforma 42, México 06048, D.F., México

**639**

Chamber of Commerce of Mexico-United States, Balderas 144 - 107, México 06070, México

**640**

FCIB/NACM (formerly Foreign Credit Interchange Bureau/National, Association of Credit Men), 520 Eighth Ave., New York, NY 10018

**641**

Federal Reserve Bank of Dallas, 400 Sakard, Dallas, TX 75202

**642**

Inter-American Council of Commerce and Production, c/o José Represas, CICYP, Homero 527, piso #7, México, D.F., México

**643**

International Business Council Mid-America, 401 North Wabash Ave., Suite 538, Chicago, IL 60611

**644**

Mexican Chamber of Commerce of the United States, 15 Park Row, Suite 1700, New York, NY 10039

**645**

National Foreign Trade Council, 100 E. 42nd St., New York, NY 10017

**645-A**

Southern Border Custom House Brokers Association, P.O. Box 698, Nogales, AZ 85628

## 1. Mexican Border Cities: Chambers of Commerce

*State of Baja California Norte*
**646**

Cámara de Comercio, Ciudad de Mexicali, Baja California Norte, México

**647**

Cámara de Comercio, Ciudad de Tijuana, Baja California Norte, México

*State of Chihuahua*

**648**

Cámara de Comercio, Ciudad Juarez, Chihuahua, Mexico

**649**

Cámara de Comercio, Ciudad de Ojinaga, Chihuahua, México,

*State of Coahuila*

**650**

Cámara de Comercio, Ciudad Acuña, Coahuila, México

**651**

Cámara de Comercio, Ciudad de Piedras Negras, Coahuila, México

*State of Sonora*

**652**

Cámara de Comercio, Ciudad de Nogales, Sonora, México

**653**

Cámara de Comercio, Ciudad de San Luis, Sonora, México,

*State of Tamaulipas*

**654**

Cámara de Comercio, Ciudad de Camargo, Tamaulipas, México

**655**

Cámara de Comercio, Ciudad de Matamoros, Tamaulipas, México

**656**

Cámara de Comercio, Ciudad de Nuevo Laredo, Tamaulipas, México

**657**

Cámara de Comercio, Ciudad de Reynosa, Tamaulpias, México

## 2. United States Border Cities: Chambers of Commerce

*Arizona*

**658**

Chamber of Commerce, City of Douglas, Douglas, AZ 85607

**659**

Chamber of Commerce, City of Nogales, Nogales, AZ 85621

**660**

Chamber of Commerce, City of Yuma, Yuma, AZ 856364

*California*

**661**

Chamber of Commerce, City of Calexico, Calexico, CA 92231

**662**

Chamber of Commerce, City of El Centro, El Centro, CA 92244

**633**

Greater San Diego Chamber of Commerce, 110 West C St., Suite 1600, San Diego, CA 92101

*Texas*

**664**

Chamber of Commerce, City of Brownsville, Brownsville, TX 78520

**665**

Chamber of Commerce, City of Del Rio, Del Rio, TX 78840

**666**

Chamber of Commerce, City of Eagle Pass, Eagle Pass, TX 78852

**667**

El Paso Chamber of Commerce, c/o City Hall, 2 Civic Center Plaza, El Paso, TX 79901

**668**

Chamber of Commerce, City of Laredo, Laredo, TX 78040

**669**

McAllen Chamber of Commerce, 10 North Broadway, P.O. Box 790, McAllen, TX 78501

**670**

Chamber of Commerce, City of Port Isabel, Port Isabel, X 78578

**671**

Chamber of Commerce, City of Presidio, Presidio, TX 79845

# B. GOVERNMENT AGENCIES

## 1. Local Level

**672**
Organization of U.S. Border Cities, c/o Chamber of Commerce of
El Paso, P.O. Box 9738, El Paso, TX 79987

## 2. State Level

*Arizona*

**673**
Project Coordinator, Federal-State Relations, Arizona Dept. of
Commerce, State Capitol, West Wing, 4th floor, 1700 W. Washington St., Phoenix, AZ 85007

*California*

**674**
Dept. of Commerce, State of California, 1121 L St., Room 600,
Sacramento, CA 95814

**675**
Dept. of Economic Development, State of California, 1121 L St.,
Room 600, Sacramento, CA 95814

**676**
Federal-State Relations Section, State Clearinghouse, Office of
Planning and Research, Office of the Governor, 1400 10th St.,
Sacramento, CA 95814

*Texas*

**677**
Economic Development Commission, Texas, Executive Director,
Box 12728, Capitol Station, Austin, TX 78711

**678**
Executive Director, Good Neighbor Commission, Box 12007, Capitol Station, Austin, TX 78711

**679**

Office of State-Federal Relations, State of Texas, P.O. Box 13005, Austin, TX 78711

**680**

Special Committee on Border Trade and Tourism, State Senate, State Capitol, 100 E. 11th St., Austin, TX 78701

### 3. National Level

**681**

International Trade Administration, U.S. Dept. of Commerce, Washington, DC 20230

**682**

President's Export Council, U.S. Dept. of Commerce, Room 3213, 14th and Constitution Ave., NW, Washington, DC 20230

**683**

International Boundary and Water Commission, United States and Mexico, Suite C-310, 4171 North Mesa St., El Paso, TX 79902

**684**

Bureau of International Labor Affairs, U.S. Dept. of Labor, 200 Constitution Ave., NW, Washington, DC 20210

**685**

Mexico-United States Interparliamentary Group, Room SH-231B, Office of Interparliamentary Services, Washington, DC 20510

**686**

Economic and Business Affairs Section, U.S. Dept. of State, 2201 C St., NW, Washington, DC 20520

*United States Consulates in Mexican Border Cities (U.S. Dept. of State), Entries 687-690:*

**687**

United States Consulate, 924 Avenida Lopez, Ciudad Juarez, Chihuahua, México

**687-A**

United States Consulate, 130 Morelia, Hermosillo, Sonora, Mexico

**688**

United States Consulate, Avenida Primera #232, Matamoros, Tamaulipas, México

**688-A**

United States Consulate, Avenida Constitución 411, Poniente 64006, Monterrey, Nuevo León, Mexico

**689**

United States Consultate, Avenida Allende 3330, Colonia Jardín, Nuevo Laredo, Tamaulipas, México

**690**

United States Consultate, Tapachula 96, Tijuana, Baja California Norte, México

**691**

U.S. Customs Service, Dept. of the Treasury, 1301 Constitution Ave., NW, Washington, DC 20229

**692**

Subcommittee on Commerce, Consumer and Monetary Affairs, Committee on Government Operations, U.S. House of Representatives, The Capitol, Washington, DC 20515

**693**

Subcommittee on Economic Stabilization, Committee on Banking, Finance and Urban Affairs, U.S. House of Representatives, The Capitol, Washington, DC 20515

**694**

U.S. International Trade Commission, 701 E St., NW, Washington, DC 20436

**695**

U.S.-Mexico Commission for Border Development and Friendship, U.S. Section, c/o Office of the President, The White House, 1600 Pennsylvania Ave., NW, Washington, DC 20500

**696**

Subcommittee on Foreign Economic Policy, Committee on Foreign Relations, U.S. Senate, The Capitol, Washington, DC 20510

**697**

Subcommittee on Multinational Corporations, Committee on Foreign Relations, U.S. Senate, The Capitol, Washington, DC 20510

### 4. Mexican Government

**698**

Secretaría de Gobernación, Francisco Espejel 92, 7 de Enero de 1907, Colonia Moctezuma, México, D.F., México (treats immigration and all domestic matters)

**699**

Secretaría del Patrimonio y Fomento Industrial (Ministry of Industrial Patrimony and Development), Av. Insurgentes Sur #552, México, D.F., México

### 5. International Level

**699-A**

UN Center on Transnational Corporations, United Nations, United Nations Plaza, New York, NY 10017

## C. INFORMATION CENTERS

**700**

Centro de Información para Asuntos Migratorios y Fronterizos (Information Center for Migration and Border Matters), American Friends Service Committee, Ignacio Mariscal #132, México 1, D.F., México

**701**

Fund for Multinational Management Education, 680 Park Ave., New York, NY 10021 (aims to provide information on the role of private U.S. corporations in international development, to industry, governments and international associations)

**702**

Michoacán Information Center on the Mexico-U.S. Future, Apartado Postal 241, Morelia 58000, Michoacán, México

**703**

U.S.-Mexico Border Program, American Friends Service Committee, 1501 Cherry St., Philadelphia, PA 19102

## D. LABOR UNIONS

**704**

AFL-CIO, 815-Sixteenth St., NW, Washington, DC 20036

**705**

Confederación de Trabajadores de México (Confederation of Workers of Mexico), Palma Norte 416, piso #4, México 1, D.F., México

**706**

Confederación General de Trabajadores (General Workers' Confederation), Dr. Río de la Loza 6, México 7, D.F., México

## E. PROFESSIONAL ASSOCIATIONS

**707**

The Business Association of Latin American Studies (BALAS), c/o Dr. Robert P. Vichas, Executive Secretary, P.O. Drawer 7638, Ft. Lauderdale, FL 33338

**708**

Committee on Mexican Studies, Conference on Latin American History, c/o Institute for Regional Study of the Californias, San Diego State University, San Diego, CA 92182

**709**

Latin American Studies Association, William Pitt Union, 9th Floor, University of Pittsburgh, Pittsburgh, PA 15260

**710**

Mexican-American Legal Defense and Educational Fund, 28 Geary St., San Francisco, CA 94108

**711**

Secretariat, U.S.-Mexico Border Health Association, Coaches Coronado Tower, 6004 North Mesa St., El Paso, TX 79912

## F. RESEARCH CENTERS

*Arizona*

**712**

Latin American Area Center, University of Arizona, Social Sciences Bldg., Room 216, Tucson, AZ 85721

*California*

**713**

Border Studies Program, San Diego State University, San Diego, CA 92182

**713-A**

Institute for Border Studies, San Diego State University-Imperial Valley, 720 Heber Ave., Calexico, CA 92231

**714**

Chicano Studies Research Center, University of California, Los Angeles, Los Angeles, CA 90024

**715**

Center for Social and Behavioral Sciences, University of California, Riverside, Riverside, CA 92521

**716**

Center for Iberian and Latin American Studies, University of California, San Diego, D-010, La Jolla, CA 92093 (studies Border topics, among other topics in broad disciplines of regions covered)

**717**

Center for U.S.-Mexican Studies, Q-057, University of California, San Diego, La Jolla, CA 92093

*Texas*

**718**

Latin American Studies Institute, Baylor University, P.O. Box 6369, Waco, TX 76706 (research on Border industry)

**719**

Mexico-United States Border Research Program, University of Texas at Austin, Austin, TX 78712

**720**

Population Research Center, University of Texas at Austin, Austin, TX 78712

**721**

School of Social Work Research Center, University of Texas at Austin, 2609 University Ave., Austin, TX 78712

**722**

Center for Inter-American and Border Studies, University of Texas at El Paso, El Paso, TX 79968

**723**

Institute of Oral History, University of Texas at El Paso, Liberal Arts Bldg., Room 339, El Paso, TX 79968 (local history, folklore)

*New Mexico*

**724**

Center for Business Services, Box 3004, New Mexico State University, Las Cruces, NM 88003

**725**

Joint Border Research Institute, New Mexico State University, Box 3JBR, Las Cruces, NM 88003

**726**

Latin American Institute, University of New Mexico, 801 Yale, N.E., Albuquerque, NM 87131 (has worked on public policy, women in development)

*New York*

**727**

North American Congress on Latin America (NACLA), 151 West 19th St., 9th Floor, New York, NY 10011 (covers Border matters, especially for economic and sociological aspects, including labor)

*Washington, D.C.*

**728**

Center for Multinational Studies, 1400 Eye St., NW, Suite 510, Washington, DC 20005 (research and information on various aspects of U.S. multinational corporations abroad)

**729**

Institute for International Economics, 11 Dupont Circle, NW, Washington, DC 20036

**730**

Overseas Development Council, 1717 Massachusetts Ave., NW, Suite 501, Washington, DC 20036

## France

**731**

Institut des Hautes Études de l'Amérique Latine, 28 rue Saint Guillaume, 75007 Paris, France (Institute of Advanced Studies for Latin America)

## Mexico

Guadalajara, Jalisco

**732**

Instituto de Estudios Sociales, Universidad de Guadalajara, Avenida Juarez 974, Sector Juarez, Guadalajara 44100, Jalisco, México (Institute for Social Studies Research)

Mexicali, Baja California Norte

**733**

Escuela de Ciencias Sociales y Políticas, Universidad Autónoma de Baja California, Apartado Postal 459, Mexicali, Baja California Norte, México (economic and political studies)

**734**

Escuela de Economía, Universidad Autónoma de Baja California, Apartado 459, Río Concho Paseo del Valle, Mexicali, Baja California Norte, México (research on Border economic matters)

Mexico, Federal District

**735**

Centro de Ecodesarrollo, Altadena 8, México 03810, D.F., México (Center for Ecological Development)

**736**

Centro de Estudios Económicos y Demográficos, El Colegio de México, Camino al Ajusco #20, Colonia Pedregal de Santa Teresa, México 1074 D.F., México (Center for Economic and Demographic Studies)

**737**

Centro de Investigación y Docencia Económicas, A.C., Carretera México-Toluca km. 16.5, Apartado 10-883, 01210 México D.F., México (economics of Border areas)

**738**

Centro de Estudios Fronterizos, El Colegio de México, Camino al Ajusco #20, Colonia Pedregal de Santa Teresa, México 1074, D.F., México (Border Studies Center)

**739**

Instituto de Investigaciones Económicas, Universidad Nacional Autónoma de México, Ciudad Universitoria, Del. Coyoacán, 04510 México, D.F., México (economic research)

**740**

Instituto Latinoamericano de Estudios Transnacionales (Latin American Institute of Trans-Border Studies), Avenida María 23, Apartado Postal 21-440, Coyoacán, México 04000 D.F., México

**741**

Instituto Nacional de Estadística, Geografía e Informática, Patriotismo 711, P.H., Colonia San Juan Mixcoac, Del. Benito Juarez, México 03730, D.F., México (National Institute on Statistics, Geography and Information Science)

**742**

Programa de Estudios de la Frontera y los Estados Unidos, El Colegio de México, Camino al Ajusco #20, México 1074, D.F., Mexico (Program of Border and U.S. Studies)

Tijuana, Baja California Norte

**743**

Centro de Estudios Fronterizos del Norte de México, Bulevar Abelardo Rodriguez 21, Zona del Río, Tijuana, B.C., Mexico (Center for Northern Mexico Border Studies)

**744**

Escuela de Economía, Universidad Autónoma de Baja California, Ejido Tampico, Ciudad Universitaria, Tijuana, Baja California Norte, México (School of Economics)

## G. ROSTER OF EXPERTS

**745**

Howard Boysen, IMEC Corporation, 3065 Beyer Blvd., San Diego, CA 92154 (establishes *maquiladoras*, for firms)

**746**

Jorge A. Bustamante, Dept. of Sociology, University of California, Riverside, Riverside, CA 92521 (political and economic aspects)

**747**

José Casar, Instituto Latinoamericano de Estudios Transnacionales, (Latin American Institute of Trans-Border Studies), Avenida María 23, Apartado Postal 21-440, Coyoacán, México 04000, D.F., México (multinational corporations, the *maquiladora*)

**747-A**

Jorge T. Castañeda, Escuela de Ciencias Políticas y Diplomáticas, Universidad Nacional Autónoma de México, Ciudad Universitaria, Del. Coyoacan, 04510 México, D.F., México (politics and economics of Border regions)

**748**

Henry V. Cisneros, Mayor, City of San Antonio, P.O. Box 9066, San Antonio, TX 78285 (Border municipal administration and economic matters)

**749**

Charles D. Dillman, Dept. of Geography, Northern Illinois University, De Kalb, IL 60115 (the *maquiladora* in general)

**750**

Paul W. Goodman, Dept. of Sociology, University of Texas at El Paso, El Paso, TX 79968

**751**

Niles M. Hansen, Dept. of Economics, University of Texas at Austin, Austin, TX 78712

**752**

Dilmus D. James, Dept. of Economics, University of Texas at El Paso, El Paso, TX 79968

**752-A**

Jerry R. Ladman, Dept. of Economics, Arizona State University, Tempe, AZ 85287

**753**

Patrick J. Lucey (former Governor of Wisconsin, and ex-Ambassador to Mexico), 315 W. Gorham St., Madison, WI 53703 (consultant, establishing *maquiladoras*)

**753-A**

Mario Margulis, El Colegio de México, Camino al Ajusco #20, Colonia Pedregal de Santa Teresa, México 1074, D.F., Mexico

**754**

Roberto Marino, Banco Nacional de México
Avenida Isabela la Católica 44, México 06089, D.F., México (economic and industrial matters)

**755**

Oscar J. Martínez, Dept. of History, University of Arizona, Tucson, AZ 85721

**756**

Lorenzo Meyer, El Colegio de México, Camino al Ajusco #20, Colonia Pedregal de Santa Teresa, México 1047, D.F., México (economics and politics of Border region)

**756-A**

Ronald Müller, Dept. of Economics, The American University, 4400 Massachusetts Ave., NW, Washington, DC 20016

**757**

Devón G. Peña, Dept. of Sociology, Colorado College, Colorado Springs, CO 80903

**758**

Jean F. Revel-Mouroz, 55 quai de Bourbon, 75004 Paris, France (Border industrialization, and *maquiladoras*)

**759**

Martin E. Rosenfeldt, Dept. of Business Administration, North Texas State University, Denton, TX 76203 (general business activities, Border region)

**760**

Mitchell A. Seligson, Dept. of Political Science, University of Arizona, Tucson, AZ 85721

**761**

Elwyn Stoddard, Dept. of Sociology and Anthropology, University of Texas at El Paso, El Paso, TX 79968 (the *maquiladora*, all aspects)

**762**

Susan B. Tiano, Dept. of Sociology, University of New Mexico, Albuquerque, NM 87131 (female labor in *maquiladoras*)

**763**

Raul Trajtenberg, Instituto Latinoamerican de Estudios Transnacionales, Avenida María 23, Apartado Postal 21-440, Coyoacán, México 04000, C.F., México

**764**

Víctor Urquidi, El Colegio de México, Camino al Ajusco #20, Colonia Pedregal de Santa Teresa, México 1074, D.F., México (Border economics)

**765**

Edward J. Williams, Political Science Dept., University of Arizona, Tucson, AZ 85721

**766**
Miguel S. Wionczek, Centro de Estudios Monetarios Latinoamericanos, and, El Colegio de México, Camino al Ajusco #20, México 1074, D.F., México

## H. UNITED STATES AND MEXICAN CITIES AND TOWNS ON OPPOSITE SIDES OF THE BORDER

| *United States* | *Mexico* |
|---|---|
| Douglas, Arizona | Agua Prieta, Sonora |
| Nogales, Arizona | Nogales, Sonora |
| Yuma-San Luis, Arizona | San Luis Potosí, Sonora |
| Calexico-El Centro, California | Mexicali, Baja California Norte |
| San Diego-San Ysidro, California | Tijuana, Baja California Norte |
| Brownsville, Texas | Matamoros, Tamaulipas |
| Del Rio, Texas | Ciudad Acuña, Coahuila |
| Eagle Pass, Texas | Piedras Negras, Coahuila |
| El Paso, Texas | Ciudad Juarez, Chihuahua |
| Laredo, Texas | Nuevo Laredo, Tamaulipas |
| McAllen, Texas | Reynosa, Tamaulipas |
| Presidio, Texas | Ojinaga, Chihuahua |
| Rio Grande City, Texas | Camargo, Tamaulipas |

# VII. Index to Directories

Note: all numbers refer to individual entries, and not to pages. All entries bearing Spanish-language names, exclusive of persons, are located in Mexico.